William S Abern...
Durham, NC
3/2024

W9-BXD-737

After the Empire

EUROPEAN PERSPECTIVES

EUROPEAN PERSPECTIVES

A Series in Social Thought and Cultural Criticism

Lawrence D. Kritzman, Editor

European Perspectives presents outstanding books by leading European thinkers. With both classic and contemporary works, the series aims to shape the major intellectual controversies of our day and to facilitate the tasks of historical understanding.

For a complete list of books in the series, see pages 235–236.

AFTER THE EMPIRE
The Breakdown of the American Order

Emmanuel Todd

Foreword by Michael Lind

TRANSLATED BY C. JON DELOGU

COLUMBIA UNIVERSITY PRESS   NEW YORK

COLUMBIA UNIVERSITY PRESS

Publishers Since 1893

New York   Chichester, West Sussex

Library of Congress Cataloging-in-Publication Data

Todd, Emmanuel, 1951–

[Après l'empire. English]

After the empire: the breakdown of the American order /

Emmanuel Todd ; translated by C. Jon Delogu.

p. cm.

Includes bibliographical references and index.

ISBN 0–231–13102–X (alk. paper)

1. United States—Foreign relations—2001–

2. Geopolitics—United States.

I. Title

E902.T63   2003

327.73—dc22   2003055599

Printed in the United States of America

c 10 9 8 7 6 5 4 3

CONTENTS

TABLES

FOREWORD

Michael Lind

At the beginning of the twenty-first century, according to the conventional wisdom, the United States of America bestrides the world like a colossus. Not since ancient Rome has a single state wielded such awesome military power. Not since the zenith of British finance has a single country so dominated the world economy. The American right celebrates the unprecedented power of America, while the left in the United States and much of the world decries it. Like it or not, the American Empire is here, and the rest of humanity must find a place in a Pax Americana that will last for generations, if not centuries.

This is all nonsense, if Emmanuel Todd is to be believed. *After the Empire: The Breakdown of the American Order* is a powerful antidote to hysterical exaggeration of American power and potential by American triumphalists and anti-American polemicists alike. A best-seller in Europe, Todd's book should be read by all thoughtful Americans for its provocative and well-informed analysis of their nation and its prospects.

There is a distinguished tradition of French thinkers, from Alexis de Tocqueville to Jean Jacques Servan-Schreiber, whose studies of the United States are really as much about France or Europe as they are about their ostensible subject. Todd does not belong in that tradition. He belongs in a different French tradition, of which Raymond Aron was the leading representative in the twentieth century, a tradition going back to the Encyclopedists—enlightened, liberal, skeptical, empirical.

Todd is a philosopher and political theorist. He is also a

demographer and student of economic trends. Because demography and economics provide the ultimate underpinnings of military and diplomatic power, Todd has far more credibility than pundits who predict the future in books that travel from the best-seller rack to the remainder box with depressing speed. He also has a track record. Following the demise of the Soviet Union, many thinkers claimed to have predicted it, just as, after the war, everyone belonged to the French Resistance. In fact very few people recognized the severity of Soviet decline; Todd was one, in his 1976 book, *La Chute finale* (*The Final Fall*, 1979).

In *After the Empire*, Todd attempts something similar not only for the United States but for the world as a whole: " . . . there will certainly not be in, say, 2050, an 'American Empire' because the United States simply does not have what it takes to be a true empire."

Todd's description of what he calls the "theatrical micromilitarism" of the United States following the Cold War will enrage the proponents of a Pax Americana—and make more thoughtful readers wince with the recognition of his accuracy: "Unable to control the real powers of its day—by holding on to Japan and Europe in the industrial sector and breaking up Russia's core and its nuclear capability—America has resorted to making a show of empire by choosing to pursue military and diplomatic actions among a series of puny powers dubbed for dramatic effect 'the axis of evil.' . . . Embargoes are put in place against defenseless countries, insignificant armies are bombarded, increasingly sophisticated armaments that are said to have the precision of video games are being conceived and built, it is claimed, and yet in practice unarmed civilian populations are bombed in old-fashioned ways that are reminiscent of World War II." These words were written before the United States, against the opposition of most of its allies and most countries in the world, invaded and occupied Iraq in order to eliminate the alleged threat of weapons of mass destruction, which, it turned out, could not be found and probably did not exist. In the summer of 2003 the U.S. military announced that two small wars and the occupation of two minor countries, Afghanistan and Iraq, had strained its manpower almost to the breaking point. So much for the "new Roman empire."

Todd understands, as the American political elite evidently does not, that military power cannot be understood apart from economic performance. For decades the United States, while exporting soldiers, has helped to promote global economic growth by importing manufactured goods and immigrants. The price has been paid by great numbers of working-class and middle-class Americans, who as a result of deindustrialization have been shoved into a poorly paid service sector proletariat at the very moment that it has been flooded by unskilled immigrants. A declining and indebted American middle class cannot serve for much longer as the market of first resort for countries trying to export their way into prosperity. Sooner or later there will be a "correction," with effects felt not only in the United States but around the world.

As this suggests, *After the Empire* is as much about trends in global society as it is about the future of the United States. Unlike many Europeans (and some Americans), Todd is not interested in pointing out the flaws of America in order to highlight the virtues of an idealized Europe. On the contrary, he sees many disturbing American phenomena—the rise of stratification based on educational credentials, the obsolescence of unreformable political institutions—as examples of trends that are manifest in many other advanced industrial democracies, including France.

After the Empire is a sympathetic critique of the United States, not an anti-American polemic. Todd has no patience with what he calls "structural anti-Americans." "But we should not be fooled by these anti-Americans whose attachment to reality and history is like that of stopped clocks, which of course tell the correct time twice a day. The most typical representatives of this group are in fact Americans. Read the texts of Noam Chomsky and you will not find the slightest awareness of the evolution of the world." Indeed, Todd argues that contemporary Europe should emulate the civilian, republican United States of the nineteenth and early twentieth centuries—not the militarized parody of the British Empire that the United States has become since the end of the Cold War. "Let us follow the example of that early successful America Let us dare to become strong by refusing militarism and concentrating instead on the economic and social problems within our societies."

The purpose of Emmanuel Todd in *After the Empire* is not denunciation but diagnosis. In spite of Todd's combination of sympathy with objectivity, the reaction of many Americans to his sobering diagnosis may be like that of a patient who, having been told by quacks he has the body of an Olympic champion, is finally informed by a genuine doctor that he has serious but not incurable health problems. In attempting to correct the exaggeration of American power and prosperity, Todd may emphasize some weaknesses too much. "There is a great deal of ruin in a country," as Adam Smith observed. But one should also bear in mind the possibility that there are design defects of the United States—cultural, as well as military, diplomatic and economic—that no one at present foresees. Only one thing can be certain—those who assume that a trend such as the growth of American power in the 1990s and 2000s (or the growth of Soviet power in the 1950s and 1960s) will continue indefinitely are certain to be wrong.

In the 1990s the Tech Bubble entranced much of America and the world. Pundits made fortunes claiming that the business cycle was over and a new age of universal prosperity had dawned. Government budgets reflected these utopian assumptions. The skeptics who pointed out that inevitably the bubble would burst were ignored. The bubble burst. In the first decade of the twenty-first century, the Empire Bubble has succeeded the Tech Bubble and will look as absurd in hindsight in a decade or two.

And after the empire? "The planet is tending toward stability after the pain of an educational and demographic transition that is nearing completion." Of all of Todd's challenges to the conventional wisdom, this is perhaps the most provocative. And here perhaps Emmanuel Todd does resemble the stereotype of the French thinker held by many in the United States and the world. What could be more Gallic in its paradoxical ingenuity than the assertion, in a time of great-power peace, when the media's sensational and selective focus on terrorism and small-scale conflicts creates an impression of ever escalating chaos, that the worst is behind us and the best may lie ahead?

PREFACE

Writing the preface to a foreign edition of a book is usually pure joy. To see the work go beyond one's own cultural system is an important moment—a sign that perhaps what one is saying is of general importance and not merely a local tribal concern. But I have to admit that I come to the task of writing the preface for the American edition of *Après l'empire* with mixed feelings. I must here address Americans on the subject of the decline of their own country, and I do not see how a normal human being could take pleasure in telling other normal human beings that their country is ill, that it has made foolish strategic choices, and that they, as Americans, must prepare for a reduction of their power and, most likely, of their standard of living.

Therefore, before examining the recent developments in international politics that have come about since the publication of this book in France, I would like to try and avoid any misunderstandings by stating "where I'm coming from" intellectually and culturally, with the hope that these biographical facts will allow the reader to evaluate the significance and direction of my work correctly. I do this even though I believe that what counts is not the identity of the author but knowing instead if his arguments are valid.

In 1976 I published a book, *La Chute finale* (*The Final Fall*, 1979), which predicted the collapse of the Soviet system. At the time I was widely labeled "anticommunist," just as, following the publication of *Après l'empire*, I was often (but not always) labeled "anti-American." Labels aside, professionally I am a historian and anthropologist trained to examine periods, places, customs, and conflicts with a cold eye. For the most part this is how I see the interpretative stance adopted in *Après l'empire*, even if now and then I allow myself to make a few moral and political remarks that reveal my European and French identity. Moreover, in my conclusion I formulate some proposals that might help resolve the planet's "America problem." The motive for writing this book, however, was not political passion but, rather, my exasperation as a historian and researcher. In the fall of 2002 I had the feeling that the world was about to repeat the same mistake with regard to the United States that it made during the 1970s with the Soviet Union: reading an expansion in military activity as a sign of increasing power when in fact it serves to mask a decline.

It would be a mistake to think of me as one more "typical French intellectual" carrying the same old anti-American virus that has infected so many Parisian intellectuals. The truth is that my family ties with the Anglo-Saxon world are numerous and long-standing. In Paris the Todd family is suspected of having a culpable preference for America and England. The suspicions are in one sense justified. My father's father, who died last year, was an American citizen of Jewish-Austrian origins. As for my mother's family, they spent the Second World War as refugees in America because of their Jewish origins. This is why up until very recently the United States has been a kind of subconscious safety net for me—the place where I could go if things went bad in Europe. This is probably the deep reason why I was until two years ago opposed to both the Maastricht Treaty on European unification and the idea of a properly European power. Given my confidence in the United States, I felt no need for another counterweight to America after the collapse of the Soviet Union. It is the recent behavior of the United States—its emergence as a major factor in the world's disorder and armed conflicts—that has made me become a good European and, by the same token, politically opposed to the United States.

Intellectually speaking, I can hardly be said to have come out of the proper French mold since I owe my training as a researcher to Cambridge University. Over the years I have remained fundamentally loyal to British empiricism. I do not mind saying that when it comes to research, I have always considered the English research tradition as stronger and more efficient than the French.

Having now spelled out who I am and what I believe, I shall comment bluntly on some of the important events that have transpired since the French publication of *Après l'empire*.

Après l'empire appeared in France at the beginning of September 2002. It was generally well received by critics, who, it seems, were not unduly worried by my announcement of the imminent breakdown of the American order. Some may even have experienced a degree of schadenfreude while imagining this prospect. In any case it must be said that the events of the past year have largely confirmed the book's main idea as well as its general prognosis concerning America's altered relation to the rest of the world. One could even say that the process outlined in the book has accelerated, as though the Bush administration were methodically pursuing a program to undermine the legitimacy of the United States abroad and destroy the American strategic system. The United States, which until very recently played an important role in building international order, appears more and more clearly to be contributing to disorder throughout the world.

The war against Iraq represents a decisive stage in this recent transformation. *Après l'empire*'s thesis about the significance of America's "theatrical micromilitarism" was all too well illustrated by the aggressive preemptive strike of the world's leading military power against a military midget—an underdeveloped country of twenty-four million inhabitants exhausted by a decade-long economic embargo. The theatrical media coverage of this war, including the U.S. military's close surveillance of how the war was "playing" back home and around the world, must not blind us to a fundamental reality: the size of the opponent chosen by the United States is the true indicator of its current power. Attacking the weak is hardly a convincing proof of one's own strength. On the contrary, and in direct confirmation of the central thesis of this book, the United States is pretending to remain the world's indispensable superpower by attacking insignificant adversaries. But this America—a militaristic, agitated, uncertain, anxious country projecting its own disorder around the globe—is hardly the "indispensable nation" it claims to be and is certainly not what the rest of the world really needs now.7

America on the other hand cannot "go it alone"—a fact that has become increasingly evident over the past twelve months. Its huge trade deficit has increased further since the publication of *Après l'empire*. Its dependence on foreign sources of investment capital is greater than ever. America's real war is about economics not terrorism. The country is battling to maintain its status as the world's financial center by making a symbolic show of its military might in the heart of Eurasia, thereby hoping to forget and have others ignore America's industrial weakness, its financial needs, and its predatory character. However, instead of reinforcing the image of America's global leadership as the current administration in Washington expected, its forced march into war has produced a rapid decline in the international status of the United States.

The war aggravated the global economic crisis that has been mismanaged by the world's central power. The American economy itself is increasingly perceived as an unfathomable mystery. One no longer has any clear idea which U.S. companies are totally genuine. One no longer knows how this economy works or what effect interest rates approaching zero will have on its various components. The economic anxiety among America's ruling class is almost palpable. Daily changes in the level of the dollar are followed nervously in the press. No one is even sure if the American economy will be able to absorb the shock of the war in Iraq that,

even though small in strictly military terms, is proving to be a serious economic burden since the "allies" no longer want to pay a
share of the costs as they did during the first Gulf war. The domestic and foreign deficits of the United States are skyrocketing.
Indeed leaders around the world are wondering more and more if
the central regulating power of the world economy is not heading
toward a sheer abandonment of the basic rules of capitalist rea-
soning. Its adventurism is not just military, it is also financial. One
can predict that in the years or months to come financial institutions in Europe and Asia with heavy investments in the United
States will lose a lot of money—the fall of the stock market being
only the first stage in the disappearance of foreign holdings in the
United States. The dollar is dropping, but no economic model
allows one to predict how low it will go since its very status as
reserve currency is becoming uncertain.

At the present time, however, the principal failure of the
United States is ideological and diplomatic. Far from being on
the verge of world domination, America is steadily losing control
throughout the world. Far from appearing as the upstanding
leader of the free world, the United States's "coalition" went to
war against Iraq despite broad UN opposition and in violation of
international law. The subsequent fall in legitimacy has been fla-
grant; however, even before trying to sell the world on the virtues
of preemptive war, the American strategic system had begun to
fall apart.

Germany, whose submissiveness was taken for granted among
American politicians and pundits, said "No" to the war—a declaration that constitutes an open movement of Europe toward
strategic autonomy. Germany's action gave France the opportunity to play an important role in delaying the American stam-
pede. The negotiations that led to Resolution 1441 concerning
Iraqi disarmament were a practical demonstration of one of the
closing proposals put forward in *Après l'empire*, namely, France's
sharing of its seat on the Security Council and its veto power with

Germany. Without Germany's opposition to the war France would not have been able to do anything.

The success of *Après l'empire*, a simultaneous best-seller in France and Germany, is itself a sign that the closer ties between the two countries are not superficial, sporadic, merely circumstantial, or narrowly governmental but are instead grounded in an emerging shared political sensibility.

The newfound harmony of the Franco-German duo is only the overall expression of the European sentiment. The will of Berlin and Paris could certainly not be exercised without at least the tacit approval of the other European nations. At the present time the governments on the periphery of the European system seem somewhat behind in their awareness of the strategic stakes of the new European entity, unlike the people themselves who demonstrated massively and in concert against the American war—a phenomenon that was equally evident in Spain, Italy, and Great Britain.

The blindness of America's media and diplomatic elite during these demonstrations was extreme. They dared call Germany isolated at the very moment when its act of independence and its commitment to peace were being applauded worldwide, thus considerably enhancing Germany's international legitimacy.

A second prediction made in *Après l'empire* has also been proved correct by recent events, namely, the closer collaboration between Europe and Russia—a rapprochement made necessary by the unsettling militaristic behavior of the United States. This rapprochement between Paris, Berlin, and Moscow could be somewhat disturbing to the countries of Eastern Europe, which have only just freed themselves from Soviet domination and now find themselves in the strange position of having joined NATO only months before the collapse of that organization. It was inevitable that Hungary, Poland, and the other countries that recently broke loose from the Soviet orbit should experience this strategic revolution with fear and would prefer to wait before throwing their lot in with France and Germany.

Russia has regained its balance in a much weakened and non-imperialist form. Its strategic interest is to form an equitable partnership with Europe. It will not take long for the former "popular democracies" to understand that the United States offers them no strategic advantage. Given its various deficiencies, America is unable to extend economic aid or protect them with anything but words. Their true security can only come through a complete commitment to Europe and their active participation in a common European defense policy. It is worth noting that the war in Iraq did not influence the important choices facing the new democracies in Eastern Europe, which one after another are voting in national referendums to join the European Union. The Iraqi conflict also allowed Russia to recover from the diplomatic isolation and low international esteem that it inherited from the Cold War and its more recent actions in Chechnya. However, the most surprising development during the buildup to America's Iraq war was the abrupt refusal of Turkey to grant territorial access to the Americans. This long-time military keystone within the NATO strategic command decided that this time its highest national interests did not include cooperation with the United States. There can be no better illustration of America's current weakness, and the root cause needs to be stressed here. After every defection of one of America's allies during the diplomatic crisis that preceded the war on Iraq, Washington was unable to force compliance or exact retribution for one simple reason: America no longer has the economic and financial resources to back up its foreign policy objectives. Due to trade surpluses, the real money has piled up in Europe and Asia, while financially speaking America has become the planet's glorious beggar. Any embargo imposed by the United States or any threat to the flow of investment capital would of course be disastrous for the world economy, but the United States would be the first to suffer, dependent as it is on the rest of the world for its supply of just about everything. This is why the American diplomatic system is falling apart little by little, and all the United States can muster in response is one bellicose action after another against minor-league powers. True power is economic power, and that is what America lacks today. The minute any major player refuses to go along and says "No" to the United States . . . surprise, nothing happens! France, for example, will not be punished because the United States does not have the means to do so. As for Germany, its financial strength is such that the United States has tried to forget that the German government and German people were among those most ardently opposed to the American war on Iraq.

(The United Kingdom did participate in the war, and its presence gave an oddly Anglo-Saxon ethnic tinge to the military coalition—something that may have further harmed America's image. Notwithstanding the ostentatious film footage of women and "people of color" in the U.S. military, it is impossible for the planet to identify with a conflict that looks very much like a war of Anglo-Saxons against Arabs. The likely behavior of the United Kingdom over the near term remains unknown. The policy of aligning itself with the American government is proving enormously destructive to the United Kingdom's international position. It must be remembered that the government's choice also meant choosing to ignore the majority of British citizens who loudly opposed the war before it began. The recent evolution of the United States has brought on a cultural and political identity crisis in Great Britain that is much more profound than the difficulties Great Britain faced with the birth of Europe. It is quite possible that the United States, whose crisis has only just begun, will itself push the British nation toward a certain weariness with America and a diplomatic and military nausea that together will lead to a change of heart and a more favorable conception of its European identity. The Europhobia of the American elite will not spare England, which in many ways represents for them the very essence of Europe, not to mention its inherently vexed status as origin-parent from which colonial America once proudly declared its independence.

The opposition of France, Germany, and Russia certainly did not prevent the war in Iraq, but for the United States it is too bad that it did not. Faced with the noncooperation of several major allies, the American government could have courageously backed down and thus avoided risking a total loss of legitimacy and leadership. Instead, it preferred rather childishly to forge ahead, according to some as a way to "save face." The United States now finds itself embroiled in Iraqi "nation-building" for an indefinite length of time. It risks losing a lot of lives, money, and time there. What is certain is that America's menacing unilateral behavior has accelerated the integration of Europe and moved the rapprochement between Europe and Russia irreversibly forward. Their combined strengths—the economic power of Europe and Russia's strategic nuclear deterrent force—will suffice to contain future American trigger-happy agitation. As for George W. Bush and his neoconservative helpers, they will go down in history as the grave diggers of the American empire.

After the Empire

Introduction

After years of being perceived as a problem solver, the United States itself has now become a problem for the rest of the world. After having been the guarantor of political freedom and economic order for half a century, the United States appears more and more to be contributing to international disorder by maintaining where it can uncertainty and conflict. It demands that the rest of the planet recognize that certain states of secondary importance constitute an "axis of evil" that must be combated and destroyed. Heading the list are the boastful but militarily insignificant Iraq of Saddam Hussein and the North Korea of Kim Chong Il, the first and last communist state to have instituted succession by primogeniture and one destined to die of old age without the least interference from the outside world. Iran, another American obsession, is a country of strategic importance but one clearly working toward a more peaceable existence both internally and internationally. Nevertheless, the American government stigmatizes it as another of the central elements within the axis of evil. The United States provoked China by bombing its embassy in Belgrade during the war in Kosovo and by stuffing a Boeing plane ordered for their leaders with easily detectable listening devices. Between three public handshakes and two nuclear disarmament agreements, America has even provoked Russia by underwriting Radio Free Europe broadcasts in Chechen, sending military advisers to neighboring Georgia, and establishing permanent, in-your-face military installations within central Asian states of the former Soviet Union. Finally, on the speculative heights of this militarist fever, the Pentagon allows documents to leak that contemplate nuclear strikes against nonnuclear countries. Washington is here applying a classic military strategy, but one not adapted to a country of its continental size: "the madman strategy" that requires appearing to one's adversaries as being capable of extreme irresponsibility in order to intimidate them. There is also the country's proposed development of a "Star Wars" missile defense shield that would upset the nuclear balance, allow the United States to rule by fear over the entire globe, and project us all into a world usually reserved for science fiction. Given all this, how can one be surprised at the new attitude of suspicion and fear that is taking hold among peoples who up to now have based their foreign policy on the reassuring axiom that the only remaining superpower was fundamentally a responsible entity?

The traditional allies and partners of the United States are made all the more nervous by the fact that they are located near those areas designated by its president as danger zones. At the same time, South Korea seizes every opportunity to repeat that it does not feel threatened by its antiquated communist neighbor to the north, just as Kuwait claims it is no longer in conflict with Iraq.

Russia, China, and Iran, three nations whose number one priority is economic development, have only one strategic goal:

resist American provocations either by ignoring them or by vocally campaigning for stability and world order—a reversal of attitude that would have seemed inconceivable ten years ago.

The leading allies of the United States are increasingly perplexed and uncomfortable. In Europe, where only France used to crow its independent views, one might be somewhat surprised to observe an irritated Germany and to see Great Britain, the longtime faithful friend, downright worried. On the other side of Eurasia, the silence of Japan is more a sign of growing discomfort than one of unqualified support.

Europeans do not understand why America refuses to resolve the Israeli-Palestinian question since it clearly has the power to do so. They are beginning to wonder if Washington might in fact be content to have a perpetual hot spot in the Middle East and to have Muslim countries express a growing hostility to the Western world.

The Al Qaeda organization, a band of mentally disturbed but ingenious terrorists, emerged from within a relatively small and circumscribed part of the planet, Saudi Arabia, even if Bin Laden and his associates recruited a few Egyptian turncoats and a handful of lost souls from the poor suburbs of Western Europe. However, America is trying to portray Al Qaeda as an omnipresent terrorist threat as evil as it is widespread—from Bosnia to the Philippines, from Chechnya to Pakistan, from Libya to Yemen—thus legitimating any punitive action it might take anywhere at anytime. The elevation of terrorism into a universal force *institutionalizes a permanent state of war across the globe*—a fourth "World War" according to certain American authors who see nothing ridiculous about considering the Cold War as the third.[1] Everything seems to indicate that the United States is, for some obscure reason, trying to maintain a certain level of international tension, a situation of limited but permanent war.

Only one year after September 11, this picture of America is paradoxical. In the hours after the terrorist attacks on the World

Trade Center, the most profound and sympathetic aspects of American dominance became apparent. It seemed to be an acceptable hegemony in a world that acknowledged the capitalist system and political democracy as the only reasonable and possible reality or goal. We clearly saw then that the principal force of America was its widely perceived legitimacy. The solidarity of the nations of the world was immediate: all condemned the attacks. The European allies expressed their solidarity with particular fervor through pledges of NATO commitments. Russia seized the moment to publicize its earnest desire to have good relations with the West. It was Russia that furnished Afghanistan's Northern Alliance with the arms it needed and opened air space within Central Asia that was essential to the deployment of American armed forces. Without the active participation of Russia, the American offensive in Afghanistan would have been impossible.

The terrorist attacks of September 11, 2001, fascinated psychiatrists: the revelation of a weakened America upset just about everyone everywhere, and not just adults but children as well. A large-scale psychological crisis shook the mental architecture of the planet within which America, the unique but legitimate superpower, had been a kind of unconscious keystone. Pro- and anti-Americans were like lost children, deprived of the authority figure they relied on to act out either their submission or their opposition. In short, the September 11 attacks revealed the voluntary character of the world's servitude.[2] Joseph Nye's theory of "soft power" was magnificently verified: America did not rule only or even chiefly through its military might but through the prestige of its values, its institutions, and its culture.[3]

Three months later the world seemed to have regained its usual equilibrium. America the conqueror had again become all-powerful thanks to its bombing campaigns. The vassals thought it safe to return to their own economic and internal affairs. Meanwhile, the usual opposition prepared to pick up where it had left off with its never-ending chants against the American empire.

And yet, one expected or at least hoped that the wounds of September 11—relatively minor if one considers the direct experiences of war by Europeans, Russians, Japanese, Chinese, or Palestinians—might bring America closer to the common lot of humanity and make it more sensitive to the problems of the poor and the weak. The world had a dream, namely that the recognition by all nations, or almost all, of the legitimate power of the United States would bring about a true empire of good in which the dominated would accept a central power and the dominant Americans would submit their authority to an idea of justice.

But it was not long before the international behavior of the United States began to be perceived differently. As the year 2002 went along, one could witness the reemergence of the same unilateral tendency that was already operative in the late nineties with Washington's refusal in December 1997 of the Ottawa treaty banning landmines and in July 1998 its refusal to go along with an accord for the establishment of an international law court. When the United States refused to approve the Kyoto agreement on air pollution controls, history seemed to be returning to an earlier pattern.

The war against Al Qaeda, which could have institutionalized the legitimacy of the United States if it had been conducted modestly and reasonably, has instead given further evidence of its growing irresponsibility. In only a few months, the image of a narcissistic, nervous, and aggressive America replaced the images of a wounded nation that was both admired and indispensable for the world's sense of balance. This is what we have come to. But where exactly does that leave us?

The most disturbing thing about the present situation is the fundamental absence of any satisfactory explanation for American behavior. Why is today's unique superpower not behaving in the good-natured and reasonable way it put into practice in the wake of World War Two? Why is it being such a destabilizing busybody? Is it because it is all-powerful? Or, on the contrary, because America feels it is losing its grip on the new world that is being born?

Before proceeding with our elaboration of a rigorous explanatory model of America's international behavior, we ought to set aside the standard image of a musclebound America whose only problem would be its excessive power. The usual anti-American chorus will therefore be of no use to us, whereas Establishment thinkers will be our surest guides.

A LOOK BACK AT THE QUESTION OF DECLINE

Structural anti-Americans offer their usual explanation: America is naughty by nature, the incarnation at the level of the state of the evils of the capitalist system. These anti-Americans are having a grand time today regardless of whether they are admirers of little local despots such as Fidel Castro or whether they have understood the total failure of state-run economies. They finally can point admonishingly to the negative role of the United States when it comes to insuring the balance and happiness of the planet. But we should not be fooled by these anti-Americans whose attachment to reality and history is like that of stopped clocks, which of course tell the correct time twice a day. The most typical representatives of this group are in fact Americans. Read the texts of Noam Chomsky and you will not find the slightest awareness of the evolution of the world. Before and after the downfall of the Soviet threat America is the same: militaristic, oppressive, and hypocritical in Iraq today as in Vietnam twenty-five years ago.[4] But America according to Chomsky is not only evil, it is all-powerful.

In a more modern "cultural studies" vein, there is Benjamin Barber's *Jihad vs. McWorld*, which paints a picture of a world ravaged by the confrontation between the contemptible spread of American culture and the no less contemptible residue of various tribalisms.[5] But the announced victory of Americanization suggests that, despite the criticisms he offers up, Barber remains at heart an American nationalist who, like Chomsky, overestimates his country's power.

In the same category of overestimation we find the notion of America as a "hyperpower" ["*hyperpuissance*"]. No matter how much respect one may have for the foreign policy of Hubert Védrine during his tenure as foreign affairs minister, we ought to admit that the concept of a "supersuperpower" tends to blind political commentators more than it enlightens them.

None of these descriptions help us understand the present situation. They presuppose a hypertrophic America, sometimes in its capacity for evil but always in terms of its power. They keep us from solving the mystery of American foreign policy, which ought to be done by exploring conditions of *weakness* not strength. The erratic and aggressive strategic path of the solitary superpower, like the precarious stagger of a drunkard, can only be fully explained by exposing unresolved or unresolvable contradictions and the feelings of inadequacy and fear that follow from them.

Reading the analyses published by the American political science establishment is more enlightening. Beyond all their differences, we can find in Paul Kennedy, Samuel Huntington, Zbigniew Brzezinski, Henry Kissinger, and Robert Gilpin the same moderate vision of an America that, far from being invincible, must cope with *the inexorable reduction of its power within a world of rising populations and economic development*. The analyses of American power vary in terms of focus: economic for Kennedy and Gilpin, cultural and religious for Huntington, diplomatic and military for Brzezinski and Kissinger. But in all of them we are presented with a disquieting representation of the strength of the United States whose power over the world appears fragile and threatened.

Despite his loyalty to realist strategic principles, and notwithstanding the admiration he maintains for his own intelligence,

Kissinger these days does not seem to possess a clear vision of the overall picture. His latest publication, *Does America Need a Foreign Policy?*, is little more than a catalog of local conflicts.[6] But in Paul Kennedy's *The Rise and Fall of Great Powers* (1988) we have a very useful portrait of an America threatened by "imperial overstretch" whereby diplomatic and military overextension is the classic result of a decrease in economic strength.[7] Samuel Huntington's *The Clash of Civilizations* (1996) is an expanded version of an article published in *Foreign Affairs* in 1993 whose tone is downright depressing.[8] Reading Huntington often feels like reading a calculated pastiche of Spengler's *The Decline of the West*. Huntington goes so far as to contest the universal spread of the English language and recommends a modest retreat of the United States back within the Catholic-Protestant block of the Western European alliance, a rejection of the Orthodox in Eastern Europe, and an outright abandonment of the two other pillars of America's strategic system, Japan and Israel, on the grounds that they are culturally too different.

Robert Gilpin's perspective combines economic and cultural considerations. It is professorial, careful, and very intelligent. Because he believes in the persistence of the nation-state, Gilpin's *Global Political Economy* perceives the underlying weaknesses of America's economic and financial systems, especially the fundamental threat of a "regionalization" of the planet. If Europe and Japan each build up their spheres of influence, they will render useless any idea of America as center of the world, and this reconfiguration will cause difficulties for the United States as it is forced to redefine its economic role.[9]

But it is Brzezinski who, in 1997, with the publication of *The Grand Chessboard*, has proven to be the most clairvoyant, despite his lack of interest in economic questions.[10] To fully comprehend his view of things, one has to rotate a globe in one's hands and take notice of the extraordinary geographic isolation of the United

States. The world's political center is in fact far from the rest of the world. Brzezinski is often accused in Europe of being a simplistic imperialist, both arrogant and brutal—and some of his strategic recommendations can cause amused or doubting smiles, as when he claims Ukraine and Uzbekistan to be crucial to American interests. However, his representation of the world's population and economy concentrated in Eurasia—a Eurasia that would be reunited after the fall of communism, and getting along without the Americans who are isolated far off in the New World—raises something of fundamental importance and seems intuitively to grasp the true threat hovering over the American system.

THE PARADOX OF FUKUYAMA: FROM AMERICA'S TRIUMPH TO AMERICA'S USELESSNESS

If we want to understand the anxiety eating away at the American Establishment, we also have to think seriously about the strategic implications for the United States of Francis Fukuyama's hypothesis of an "end of history." This theory, which dates from the late eighties and early nineties, was a source of amusement among Paris intellectuals who were surprised at Fukuyama's simplistic and easily digested reading of Hegel. History would be teleological after all, and its goal is the universalization of liberal democracy.[11] Thus, the fall of communism would be only the latest stage in this march toward human liberty, following another important stage, namely the fall of dictatorships in southern Europe (Portugal, Spain, Greece). The emergence of democracy in Turkey and the democratic progress of Latin America are also inscribed within this movement. This model of history, proposed at the very moment of the fall of the Soviet Union, was received in France as further evidence of America's typical naïveté and optimism. For those who remembered the real Hegel, living under Prussian domination, respectful of Lutheran authoritarianism to the point of worshiping the state, this portrait of him as a democratic individualist seemed laughable. Fukuyama offers us a Hegel softened by the makeup artists of Disney studios. One should also remember that Hegel was interested in the advancement of mind through history, but Fukuyama, even when he is talking about education, always privileges economic factors and seems often closer to Marx, someone who had a rather different idea about the end of history.[12] The secondary character of educational and cultural development makes Fukuyama a rather odd Hegelian, one certainly contaminated by the madness of economic determinism within American intellectual life.

These reservations aside, however, one ought to concede that Fukuyama offers a lively and pertinent empirical glance at contemporary history. To claim as early as 1989 that the universalization of liberal democracy was becoming a possibility worth examining was certainly a major achievement. European intellectuals, on the whole less in touch with the future movement of history, were at the time interested in putting communism on trial and thus concentrated on analyzing the past. Fukuyama had the bright idea to speculate about the future, a more difficult task but also a more useful one. My own belief is that Fukuyama's vision gets some things right but does not fully grasp the impact of education and demographics as contributing factors toward a stabilization of the planet.

Fukuyama includes in his theoretical model the law put forward by Michael Doyle in the early eighties, and derived more from Kant than from Hegel, which states that a war between liberal democracies is impossible.[13] Doyle offers here a second example of Anglo-Saxon empiricism, naïve in appearance but productive in practice. That war is impossible between democracies is verified by an examination of the historical record. This "proves" that while liberal democracies are not exempt from entering into wars with opposed systems, they never fight amongst themselves.

Modern liberal democracy is everywhere tending toward peace. One can hardly reproach the French and British democracies of 1933–1939 for their bellicose nature, and one can only point out with regret the isolationism of the American democracy up until Pearl Harbor. Without denying the nationalist elements within France and Great Britain before 1914, one must admit that it was the Austro-Hungarian empire and Germany, places where the policy-makers were not in practice accountable to their parliaments, that dragged Europe into the first World War.

Common sense alone would suggest that a people with a certain level of education and a satisfactory standard of living would be unlikely to elect a parliamentary majority capable of declaring a major war. Two peoples similarly organized will inevitably find a peaceful solution to their differences. But the uncontrollable clique that, by definition, directs a system that is neither democratic nor open, has much more latitude to initiate hostile action and override the desire for peace of the majority of ordinary people.

If one adds Fukuyama's universalization of liberal democracy to Doyle's impossibility of war between democracies, one gets a planet of perpetual peace.[14]

A cynic raised in the old European tradition will smile and recall man's eternal and relentless capacity to do evil and make war. But let us not stop at this objection and instead examine the argument further. What might be the implications of such a model for America? Its specialty within the world has become, by a series historical accidents, the defense of a democratic principle perceived as being under threat: by Nazi Germany, by militaristic Japan, and by communist regimes in Russia and China. The Second World War and then the Cold War have institutionalized, as it were, this historical function of America. But if democracy triumphs everywhere, we arrive at a paradoxical endpoint wherein the United States would be of no further use to the rest of the world as a military power and would have to accept being no more than one democracy among others.

This uselessness is one of the two fundamental anxieties of Washington and one of the keys for understanding the foreign policy of the United States.)As is frequently the case, the leaders of American diplomacy have formulated this new fear in terms of an inverse affirmation. In February of 1998 President Clinton's Secretary of State, Madeleine Albright, attempted to justify a missile attack on Iraq by defining the United States as "the indispensable nation."[15] As Sacha Guitry used to say, the opposite of the truth is already very close to the truth. To claim officially that the United States is indispensable implies that the question of America's purpose or usefulness in the world is already on the table. By means of these quasi-Freudian slips, government leaders are indirectly expressing the worries of strategic analysts. Madeleine Albright was stating in the form of denegation the Brzezinski doctrine that clearly perceives a marginal, isolated United States situated far from a highly populated and hard-working Eurasia where most of the history in a newly pacified world may be written.

At bottom Brzezinski accepts the threat implicit in the Fukuyama paradox and proposes a series of diplomatic and military techniques for keeping control of the Old World. Huntington's game is less straightforward: he does not accept the universalizing of shared feelings that forms the heart of Fukuyama's model and refuses to entertain the idea of democratic values and liberal economic systems spreading over the entire planet. He clings to a religious and ethnic categorization of peoples, the majority of which would be, by nature, incapable of following the Western model.

At this stage in our reflection we need not choose among diverse historical possibilities: Is liberal democracy generalizable? If so, does it bring peace? But we ought to see that Brzezinski and Huntington are responding to Fukuyama, and that the marginalization of the United States, as surprising as that idea may sound at a time when the entire world is worried about U.S. omnipotence, is haunting America's elite class. Far from contemplating a return to isolationism, America is now afraid of isolation, of finding itself alone in a world that no longer needs it. But why is it now afraid of the distance from the world that has been its *raison d'être* from the Declaration of Independence in 1776 to Pearl Harbor in 1941?

FROM SELF-RELIANCE TO ECONOMIC DEPENDENCE

(This fear of becoming useless, and of the isolation that could follow, is not just something new for American thinking, it amounts to the exact opposite of its customary position. America's separation from a corrupt Old World is one of the country's founding myths, and perhaps the most important one. As a land of freedom, abundance, and moral perfectionism, the United States set out to develop independently from Europe and to avoid the degrading conflicts of the cynical nations of the Old World.

American isolation during the nineteenth century was, however, really only diplomatic and military, since the economic growth of the United States benefited from two continuous and indispensable ingredients from Europe: capital and labor. European investment and the immigration of a largely literate workforce were two economic mainsprings of the American experience. As a result, by the end of the nineteenth century, America had the most powerful and self-reliant economy on the planet. with massive levels of production of raw materials (coal, oil, steel, etc.) and a huge trade surplus.>

At the beginning of the twentieth century the United States no longer needed the rest of the world. If one keeps in mind its actual power at the time, the first American interventions in Asia and Latin America were modest affairs. But from the First World War on, the rest of the world needed the United States. America mostly resisted this call up until 1917. Then it again chose isolation by refusing to sign the Treaty of Versailles. It was not until

Pearl Harbor and the German declaration of war that the United States would start down the path that would lead to the globally dominant military position that corresponded to its preeminent economic status.

In 1945 the American gross national product represented more than half of all production in the world, and the overwhelming effect of this was automatic and immediate. It is true that by 1950 communism covered most of Eurasia, from East Germany to North Korea; but American naval and air power had strategic control over the rest of the planet and benefited from the support of a multitude of allies and trading partners whose first priority was to combat the Soviet system. Most of the world consented to the rise of American hegemony, despite the patches of sympathy for communism among peasants, the working class, and many intellectuals.

If we want to understand recent turns of events, we must first admit that this hegemony was beneficial for several decades. Not to recognize the generally favorable character of American domination from 1950 to 1990 makes it impossible to grasp the importance of the subsequent reversal of the United States from useful to useless, as well as the difficulties, for Americans and the rest of us, that have resulted from it.

The hegemony over the noncommunist part of the globe during the years 1950 to 1990 almost deserves the name "empire." The economic, military, and ideological resources of the United States seemed for a time to be on the scale of an imperial power. The preeminence of the principles of free market economies in areas controlled politically or militarily by Washington finally transformed the world. Today we call it "globalization." Over time these economic transformations have also deeply affected the internal structure of the dominant nation, weakening its economy and deforming its society. The process was at first slow but steady. Without being fully recognized by the principal actors in this historical drama, a relation of dependence has now sprung up between the United States and its sphere of influence. An

American trade deficit appeared in the early seventies and has since become a basic structural element of the world economy.

The fall of communism has entailed a dramatic acceleration of the progression of dependence. Between 1990 and 2000 the American trade deficit went from 100 billion to 450 billion dollars. To balance its foreign accounts, America requires an equivalent flow of foreign capital into the country. At the start of this third millennium the United States is unable to subsist on its own production. At the very moment when the rest of the world — now undergoing a process of stabilization thanks to improvements in education, demographics, and democracy — is on the verge of discovering that it can get along without America, *America is realizing that it cannot get along without the rest of the world.* >

The debate about "globalization" ["*mondialisation*"] is in part disconnected from reality because we too often accept the orthodox representation of commercial and financial exchanges as being symmetrical and homogeneous, without any country occupying a particular spot. The abstract notions of labor, profit, and the free circulation of capital all mask a fundamental element: the specific role of the most important nation in the new organization of the world economy. If the United States has greatly declined in relative terms as an economic power, it has nevertheless succeeded in massively increasing its capacity to siphon off wealth from the world economy. Objectively speaking, America has become a predator; but should this situation be interpreted as a sign of strength or of weakness? This can be debated, but it is certain that America is going to have to fight politically and militarily in order to sustain the hegemony that has become indispensable for maintaining its standard of living.

This turnaround when it comes to who is relying on whom in the world economy is the second major factor, which, along with the first—the proliferation of democracies—allows one to explain the unfamiliar situation in the world at present, especially the bizarre behavior of the United States and the bewilderment of the planet. *How does one deal with a superpower that is economically dependent but also politically useless?*

We could stop our elaboration of this troubling explanatory model here and remind ourselves that the United States is after all a democracy and that democracies do not go to war amongst themselves, and therefore the United States is incapable of becoming an aggressive, warmongering danger for the rest of the world. Through trial and error the government in Washington will find the paths to economic and political adaptation within this new world. Why not? Nevertheless, we should also remember that the crises within advanced democracies—ever more visible and disquieting, especially in America—do not permit us to conclude that the United States is pacific by nature.

History does not end. Amidst the emergence of democratic functioning across the planet we should not forget that the oldest democracies—the United States, Great Britain, France—continue to evolve. Everything seems to indicate that the latter are transforming into oligarchical systems. The concept of "inversion," which has been useful for understanding the economic reversal of the United States with respect to the rest of the world, can also help us analyze the democratic dynamic in the world: democracy is progressing in those places where it was weak, but it is regressing in those where it was formerly strong.

THE DEGENERATION OF AMERICAN DEMOCRACY AND THE POSSIBILITY OF WAR

The strength of Fukuyama is to have very quickly identified a process of stabilization within the non-Western world. But his perception of societies, as we have seen, remains overly influenced by economic determinism. He does not see education as a central factor within history and is only slightly interested in demography. He does not appreciate that the literacy of the masses is the independent explanatory variable at the heart of the advances in democracy and individualism that he detects. His big mistake is to posit an end of history based on an alleged generalization of liberal democracies. His conclusion presupposes that this form of government is stable if not perfect and that its history ends the moment it is has been achieved. But what if democracy is merely the political superstructure of a particular cultural stage—simple mass literacy? In that case, continuing advances in teaching and learning at the secondary and postsecondary levels will necessarily upset democracy in the places where it first appeared.

Secondary education and especially higher education reintroduce the notion of inequality into the mental and ideological organization of developed societies. After a brief period of hesitation and scruples, the more highly educated ["*éduqués supérieurs*"] wind up believing that they are truly superior. In developed countries a new class is emerging that comprises roughly 20 percent of the population in terms of sheer numbers but controls about half of each nation's wealth. This new class has more and more trouble putting up with the constraint of universal suffrage.

Advances in literacy made us live for a time in the world of De Tocqueville for whom the march of democracy was "*providentielle*"—almost an effect of divine will. The rise of higher education today is leading us toward the calamity of another kind of "providence": oligarchy. It is a surprising return to the world of Aristotle in which oligarchy may succeed democracy.

At the very moment when democracy is beginning to take hold in Eurasia, it is weakening in those places where it was born. American society is changing into a fundamentally unegalitarian system of domination, a phenomenon perfectly conceptualized by Michael Lind in *The Next American Nation*.[16] Of particular note in his book is the first systematic description of the new postdemocratic American ruling class: "the overclass."

On a more modest scale France is nearly as far along as the United States in this area. These are indeed curious "democracies" in which the political systems pit elitism against populism and vice versa; and although universal suffrage persists in theory, in practice the elites of the right and the left close ranks to block any reorientation of economic policies that would lead to greater equality. It is an increasingly bizarre universe when after gargantuan, media-saturated campaigns the voting game ends up merely extending the status quo. The entente cordiale among the elite, a reflection of the existence of a common "superior" language among them, prohibits any cracking of the political system's façade, even when universal suffrage would seem to suggest the possibility of a crisis. George Bush was chosen as president of the United States at the end of an opaque electoral process that makes it impossible to say whether he won arithmetically. Only a short time later in France, the other grand historical republic, one saw just the opposite scenario — thus affirming the odd logic of Sacha Guitry about the identity of opposites. In France we have a president chosen by 82 percent of the voters. However, the near unanimity of the French people is the result of a sociological and political lockout of the aspirations of the lowest 20 percent ["20% d'en bas"] by the highest 20 percent ["20% d'en haut"] who also for the moment hold sway ideologically over the 60 percent in the middle.[17] But in both cases the result is the same: the electoral process is of no practical importance and the levels of voter turnout spiral inevitably downward.

In Great Britain the same mechanisms of cultural restratification are at work. They were analyzed early on by Michael Young in his brief but truly prophetic study, *The Rise of the Meritocracy* (1958).[18] But England's democratic phase was moderate and belated. Given its recent aristocratic past, which lives on in the classification system of highly readable accents and other class markers, England's transition toward the new world of Western oligarchy can proceed smoothly. In fact the new American over-class looks toward England with some envy. This explains their Anglophile stance and a nostalgia for a Victorian past that is not theirs.[19]

It would thus be inaccurate and unfair to claim that the crisis of democracy concerned only the United States. Great Britain and France, the two old liberal nations linked historically to the American democracy, are engaged in parallel processes of oligarchical aging. But within the newly globalized political and economic system, they are among the dominated and therefore obliged to pay attention to their international trade balances. Eventually the paths of their social evolution will at some point separate from that of the United States. Thus I do not think that one day we will be able to speak of the "Western oligarchies" as we have spoken in the past of the "Western democracies."

This is then the second major turnaround that explains the strained relations between the United States and the rest of the world. The progress of democracy around the world is masking the weakening of democracy in its birthplace. This turnaround is ill perceived by the actors on the world stage. America is still affable and articulate, more out of habit than cynicism, when it comes to mouthing the language of liberty and equality. And of course the democratization of the planet is far from being fully realized.

However, this passage of the United States into a new oligarchical stage cancels any application of the Doyle law concerning the inevitably peaceful consequences of the spread of liberal democracy. We can well imagine the possibility of aggressive behavior on the part of a poorly supervised ruling class, as well as a more adventurous military policy. In truth, if the hypothesis of an America tending toward oligarchy permits us to limit the validity of the Doyle law, it also keeps us from denying or doubting the empirical reality of an aggressive America. We cannot even rule out the strategic hypothesis of American aggression toward other democracies, new or old. This way of looking at the world has the merit of harmonizing, in a rather sly way it's true, both the Anglo-Saxon "idealists," who are expecting the spread of liberal democracy to bring an end to military conflict, and their "realist" counterparts, who conceive of international relations as an anarchic space occupied by aggressive states fighting each other for all eternity. If we grant the idea that liberal democracy leads to peace, we must also grant that its withering away could lead back to war. Even if the Doyle law is true, there will be no perpetual peace in the Kantian spirit.

AN EXPLANATORY MODEL

In what follows I am going to develop an explanatory model whose form is somewhat paradoxical but whose principal parts can be summarized quite easily: at the very moment when the world is discovering democracy and learning to get along politically without the United States, the United States is beginning to lose its democratic characteristics and is discovering that it cannot get along without the rest of the world.

The planet is therefore faced with a double reversal: first, the new economic dependence of the United States vis-à-vis the rest of the world and second, the new distribution of democratic energy around the world, henceforth positive in Eurasia and negative in America.

Once these large-scale sociohistorical processes have been posited, one can understand the apparent strangeness of recent American actions. Since a free and democratic order is slowly being sapped of its substance within the United States, the country's goal can hardly be to defend such an order abroad. What has become of prime importance is supplying the country with various commodities and capital. From now on the fundamental strategic objective of the United States will be political control of the world's resources.

However, the declining economic, military, and ideological power of the United States does not allow the country to master effectively a world that has become too vast, too populous, too literate, and too democratic. The subordination of the real obstacles to American hegemony—namely the strategic players Russia, Europe, and Japan—is simply too big a job to be an accessible objective. America is having to negotiate with these three and very often yield to them. But America has to find a solution, real or fanciful, for its worrisome economic dependence. The country has to remain at least symbolically at the center of the world, and to do so it will have to parade its super power, or rather its "supersuperpower." We are thus witnessing the development of a global theater of dramatized militarism that consists of three essential principles. First, never resolve a problem once and for all, so as to justify endless rounds of military action throughout the world by the one and only superpower. Second, concentrate one's energy on minor league powers such as Iraq, Iran, North Korea, Cuba, etc. The only way to remain at the heart of world affairs is to challenge small-time actors in such a way that will reflect well on American might and thereby avoid or at least delay the moment when the other major powers wake up to their role as global partners with the United States, those powers being Europe, Japan, and Russia in the near-term, and eventually China. Third, develop new arms systems that can be advertised as putting the United States far ahead of the field in an arms race that must never end.

Such a strategy certainly makes the United States a new and unexpected obstacle to world peace, but it is not one of truly threatening proportions. The list and the size of those named as adversaries gives an objective indication of America's power, since it is incapable of challenging any country more powerful than Iraq, Iran, North Korea, or Cuba. There is no reason to denounce or become hysterical about the emergence of an American empire that in reality, and only one decade after the breakup of the Soviet Union, is going through its own disintegration.

1

The Myth of Universal Terrorism

A catastrophic view of the world has dominated Western percep-
tions in the last ten to fifteen years. Day after day, the media have
constructed the image of a world organized by hatred and ravaged by violence, a world where the massacre of individuals and
whole peoples occurs at an accelerating pace: the Rwandan
genocide, religious conflicts in Nigeria and the Ivory Coast, tribal
disputes in Somalia, indescribable civil war in Sierra Leone,
gangsterism and rape in South Africa despite the end of
apartheid, assassination of white farmers in Zimbabwe, mass terrorism in Algeria. Changing continents, we find an Islamic revolution in Iran—even though somewhat more peaceful these
days—the conflict in Chechnya, anarchy in the Republic of
Georgia, a war between Armenia and Azerbaijan over possession
of the Upper Karabakh, the independence movements of Kurds
in Turkey and Iraq, civil war in Tajikistan, violence in the dis-

puted Kashmir region of India bordering Pakistan, Tamil upris-
ings in Sri Lanka, confrontations between Hindus and Muslims
in Gudjarat, a Muslim guerrilla movement south of the Philippines, Islamic radicalism in Aceh, north of Sumatra, the massacre
of East Timor Christians by Indonesian special forces, and the
grotesque regime of the Taliban in Afghanistan. With the exception of leftist hostage taking in Columbia and the revolt of the
minor military leader Marcos in Mexico, Latin America appears
exceptionally peaceful. Lately the historically violence-ridden
continents of Central and South America even compare favor-
ably with Europe where the breakup of Yugoslavia and the massacres of Croatians, Bosnians, Serbs, and Kosovars have given the
impression that a rising tide of violence was going to invade the
rich, old peaceful world of Western Europe. It would be unfair
not to mention the Chinese crackdown against student demonstrations in Tiennamen Square in 1989. And let us not forget the
height of human folly playing itself out in the endless violence
between Israelis and Palestinians. To complete our list, let us
remember the fall of the World Trade Center towers, a crime
committed in the name of Allah by suicide bombers who origi-
nated from places that we used to call the Third World.

My list is certainly no more complete than the media accounts
one receives on any given day. However, it is difficult not to come
away from such a litany of death-saturated events without feeling
that the world has gone mad and that the French live in one of
the last remaining peaceful corners of the globe—unless, that is,
one wants to view the torching of cars in the suburbs, attacks
against Parisian synagogues in the spring of 2002, and the alarm-
ing success around the same time of the far-right candidate Jean-
Marie Le Pen in the last presidential election as signs of a creep-
ing barbarization of the West.[1]

These representations of a world wracked by violence encourage one to view history through the particular lens of regression.
All of these mass killings can mean only one thing: the planet is

floundering, development is failing, and the idea of "progress" must be filed away along with other expired concepts on the shelf marked "Quaint Illusions of Eighteenth-Century Europe."

Certain areas of genuine regression in recent years can be rigorously documented. Beyond the shocking images of television "news," it is possible to measure the slowdown of economic growth in the world and the widening of inequalities in both rich and poor countries. These are some of the consequences of economic and financial globalization. They follow logically from the free-market system that makes the working populations of every country in the world into global competitors. As a result salaries eventually stop growing or collapse and global demand stagnates. Moreover, the system tends to introduce into every society a level of inequality that corresponds to the revenue gap between the richest of the rich countries and the poorest of the poor. Nevertheless, if one refuses to fall into simplistic economic schemas, whether of the left or the right, Marxist or neoconservative, there exists an immense amount of statistical information that allows one to take stock of an enormous cultural advancement going on in the world at the present time. Increases in general literacy and the spread of lower birth rates are the two fundamental changes shaping this cultural progress.

THE CULTURAL REVOLUTION

Between 1980 and 2000, the percentage of those aged fifteen and up who could read and write went from 40 percent to 67 percent in Rwanda, from 33 percent to 64 percent in Nigeria, from 27 percent to 47 percent in The Ivory Coast, from 40 percent to 63 percent in Algeria, from 77 percent to 85 percent in South Africa, from 80 percent to 93 percent in Zimbabwe, and from 85 percent to 92 percent in Columbia. Even in Afghanistan the literacy rate increased from 18 percent to 47 percent over the same twenty-year period. In India it went from 41 percent to 56 percent, in Pakistan from 28 percent to 43 percent, in Indonesia from 69 percent to 87 percent, in the Philippines from 89 percent to 95 percent, in Sri Lanka from 85 percent to 92 percent, and in Tajikistan from 94 percent to 99 percent. In the twenty years since the beginning of the Islamic revolution in Iran in 1980, the literacy rate increased from 51 percent to 77 percent. In China the literacy rate was already at 66 percent in 1980. Today it stands at 85 percent. Every poor country now seems engaged in a general race for cultural development. Even in the most "backward" places such as Mali or Niger one sees literacy growing in one generation from 14 percent to 40 percent and 8 percent to 16 percent, respectively. The overall percentage is small; however, among those aged fifteen to twenty-four, the literacy rate is 22 percent in Niger and 65 percent in Mali.

The process is not complete and the levels of cultural development still vary widely. But one can begin to see in a not too distant future a totally literate world. If one assumes that the process is likely to accelerate, we can imagine that among the younger generations universal literacy will be achieved by 2030. The invention of writing dates from somewhere around 3000 B.C. — it will therefore have taken man about five thousand years to fully accomplish the revolution linked to the written word.

LITERACY AND GLOBALIZATION

The basic skills of reading, writing, and arithmetic are only one aspect of the revolution in thinking that has spread over the entire planet. When man knows how to read, write, and count, he begins quite naturally to exert greater control over his material environment. Economic development in Asia and Latin America today is linked almost automatically to educational development just as it was in Europe between the seventeenth century and the beginning of the twentieth. In the context of free trade and global finance, economic growth is slowed and modified, but it exists. Americans, Europeans, and the Japanese ought to know that opening factories overseas in low salary areas would not have been possible without the educational gains of local populations in Brazil, Mexico, China, Thailand, or Indonesia.

The workers of the former "Third World" whose lower salaries cause havoc for workers in America, Europe, and Japan, know how to read, write, and count and that is why they can be usefully exploited. Factories are never transferred to places where the educational process has not yet reached a certain critical stage, such as in Africa for example. Economic globalization is a time sensitive principle: it seeks to maximize profits within the context of a specific moment in world history. The present context features a relative abundance of literate workers outside the major centers of earlier industrial development.

We must also keep in mind the importance of education when it comes to understanding the present waves of migration toward Europe and the United States. Individuals who are rushing to get through the guarded gates of the richest countries are no doubt trying to escape from the material misery that still exists in the world's poorest countries. But their desire to flee this misery also reveals a higher level of sophistication in their aspirations that is a direct result of substantial increases in basic literacy attained in their home countries. The consequences of education are innumerable. One of them is the psychological disorientation of populations.

THE DEMOGRAPHIC REVOLUTION

Once man, or more precisely women begin to know how to read and write, birth control can begin. Today's world, which is headed towards achieving total literacy around 2030, is also in the process of completing a demographic transformation. In 1981 the average birth rate in the world was 3.7 children per woman. This rate would have led to a rapid expansion of the world's population and have proven likely the idea of a persistent "Third World" of underdevelopment. In 2001, the average worldwide birth rate had fallen to 2.8 children per woman, a rate that is approaching the 2.1 rate of "zero population growth" that guarantees a simple one-for-one stability of the population. These numbers allow one to predict that some time in the near future, perhaps around 2050, the world's population will achieve a stable equilibrium between births and deaths.

When one examines the specific birth rates country by country, it is striking to notice that the numbers no longer establish a clear border between developed and undeveloped countries.

Table 1 shows the birth rates in 1981 and 2001 of a number of the most populated and most important countries in the world. Many of them have birth rates that fall somewhere between 2 and 3 children per woman. Some countries that not too long ago were classified as "Third World" have birth rates close to those of the major Western countries. For example, China and Thailand with birth rates of 1.8 children per woman rank between France (1.9) and Great Britain (1.7). Iran, one of the countries within the "axis of evil," went from 2.6 births per woman in 2001 to 2.1 in 2002, and thus has the same birth rate as the United States, the self-proclaimed leader of a supposed "axis of good."

This demographic revolution has not been completed everywhere. One notices Bolivia, for example, with a birth rate of 4.2. Similarly, a part of the Muslim world and the majority of the African continent still have high birth rates. However, with the exception of marginal countries such as Niger and Somalia, one notices that even in Africa the trend toward lower birth rates has begun. The trend is quite far along in the majority of Muslim countries.

TABLE 1. Fertility Rates Around the World
(Number of Children per Woman)

	1981	2001
United States	1.8	2.1
Canada	1.8	1.4
Great Britain	1.9	1.7
France	1.9	1.9
Germany	1.3	1.3
Italy	1.7	1.3
Spain	2.5	1.2
East Germany	1.9	
Romania	2.5	1.3
Poland	2.3	1.4
Russia	2.0	1.2
Ukraine	1.9	1.1
Japan	1.8	1.3
China	2.3	1.8
Taiwan	2.7	1.7
South Korea	3.2	1.5
North Korea	4.5	2.3
Vietnam	5.8	2.3
Thailand	3.7	1.8
The Phillippines	5.0	3.5
India	5.3	3.2
Sri Lanka	3.4	2.1
Argentina	2.9	2.6
Mexico	4.8	2.8
Bolivia	6.8	4.2
Peru	5.3	2.9
Brazil	4.4	2.4
Columbia	3.9	2.6
Venezuela	4.9	2.9
South Africa	5.1	2.9
Rwanda	6.9	5.8
Zambia	6.9	6.1
Zimbabwe	6.6	4.0
Kenya	8.1	4.4
Tanzania	6.5	5.6
Ethiopia	6.7	5.9
Zaire	6.1	7.0
The Ivory Coast	6.7	5.2
Sierra Leone	6.4	6.3
Liberia	6.7	6.6

SOURCE: *Population et sociétes*, September 1981, July–August 2001, n. 151 and 370, INED.

A study of birth rates shows that the Muslim world, at least as a demographic block, does not exist. Among Muslim countries one notices the greatest divergence of birth rates from 2.0 births per woman in Azerbaijan to 7.5 in Niger. The Islamic world is a microcosm of the transitions of so-called Third World countries around the globe. The former Soviet republics in the Caucasus region and in Central Asia gained high literacy levels under communism and are therefore in the lead with birth rates of 2.0 for Azerbaijan and 2.7 for Uzbekistan. Tunisia is quite far along with a rate of 2.3, which is lower than the 3.1 one finds in Algeria or the 3.4 in Morocco. In general the Maghreb region colonized by France has lowered its birth rates faster than other areas of the Middle East that constitute the heart of the Arab world and were less directly influenced by the colonial hand of Europe.

Those who consider getting control over birth rates to be one of the keys to progress can see from these numbers that France has been a positive influence in northern Africa and Russia an even more decisive influence in Central Asia. As Youssef Courbage has shown, the French influence was subtle, the result of a complex network of back and forth migrations and contact with metropolitan France. The Russian influence was clear and direct—the Soviet Union pursued a policy of total literacy across its territory, a vast project never before attempted by any other colonial power. The communist variety of colonialism did therefore have some positive aspects.

Non-Arab Muslim countries such as Turkey, at 2.5 in 2001 and Iran, at 2.1 in 2002, though never colonized, have nearly achieved their demographic transformation. If one looks even further from the Arab world to countries with more recent Islamic traditions, one notices that Indonesia and Malaysia have also nearly completed their demographic transformation with birth rates in 2001 of 2.7 and 3.2 respectively[2]

In a certain number of Muslim countries, the control over reproduction is only just beginning and one notices many birth

TABLE 2. Fertility Rates in Muslim Countries
(Number of Children per Woman)

	1981	2001
Azerbaijan	3.1	2.0
Turkmenistan	4.8	2.2
Tunisia	5.0	2.3
Kyrgyzstam	4.1	2.4
Takolostan	5.6	2.4
Lebanon	4.7	2.5
Turkey	4.3	2.5
Iran	5.3	2.6
Indonesia	4.1	2.7
Uzbekistan	4.8	2.7
Bahrain	7.4	2.8
Algeria	7.3	3.1
Malaysia	4.4	3.2
Bangladesh	6.3	3.3
Morocco	6.9	3.4
Egypt	5.3	3.5
United Arab Emirates	7.2	3.5
Jordan	4.3	3.6
Libya	7.4	3.9
Qatar	7.2	3.9
Syria	7.2	4.1
Kuwait	7.0	4.2
Sudan	6.6	4.9
Iraq	7.0	5.3
Pakistan	6.3	5.6
Saudi Arabia	7.2	5.7
Senegal	6.5	5.7
Nigeria	6.9	5.8
Palestine	6.9	5.9
Afghanistan	6.9	6.0
Mauritania	6.9	6.0
Oman	7.2	6.1
Mali	6.7	7.0
Yemen	7.0	7.2
Somalia	6.1	7.3
Niger	7.1	7.5

SOURCE: *Population et sociétés*, September 1981, July–August 2001, n. 151 and 370, INED.

rates remain above five, such as in Iraq (5.6), Pakistan (5.7), Saudi Arabia (5.8), and Nigeria (5.8).[3] The high birth rate of Palestine (5.9) is a sociological and historical anomaly—combat reproduction linked to the occupation—for which an analogous situation can also be noted in the Jewish population of Israel whose high birth rate is the exception among highly educated Western societies. The statistical evidence shows clear divisions within the Jewish population, since nonpracticing Jews and religiously moderate Jews show a birth rate of 2.4 while the Orthodox and ultra-Orthodox have a birth rate of 5.0, an increase, in fact, over the 1981 birth rate.[4]

There are still a number of Muslim countries where the demographic changes have not really happened yet and one notices birth rates above six per woman, such as in Afghanistan (6), Mauritania (6), Mali (7), Somalia (7.3), and Niger (7.5). However, the rise in literacy rates in these countries guarantees that they will follow the same path as the rest of the world toward mastery over their own reproduction.

THE CRISIS OF TRANSITION

Taken together, the progress in basic literacy and the increasing control over birth rates suggest a more positive moment in the history of the world than the dispiriting picture offered by television news reports. These two factors show humanity winning the struggle to extract itself from chronic underdevelopment. Keeping them in mind would not just be cause for optimism but would offer legitimate grounds for celebrating man's passage into a higher stage of development.

The mass media, however, are not responsible for our deformed vision of history. Progress is not, as Enlightenment thinkers may have believed, a pleasurable linear ascent on all fronts. Being uprooted from one's traditional life—from the well-trodden routines of illiteracy, pregnancy, poverty, sickness, and death—can at first produce as much suffering and disorientation as it does hope and opportunity. Very often, perhaps in a majority of cases, the transformation of cultural and personal horizons is experienced as a social and individual crisis. Destabilized peoples behave violently both among themselves and toward others. The move into modernity is frequently accompanied by an explosion of ideological violence.

This phenomenon appeared first in Europe not in the Third World. Most European nations, which are today so peaceful, went through a phase of brutal and bloody ideological adjustment. The values expressed varied widely. Liberal and egalitarian during the French Revolution, egalitarian and authoritarian during the Russian Revolution, authoritarian and inegalitarian in the case of Nazi Germany. And one should not forget England, a model of reason but nevertheless the continent's first revolutionary nation, which began its move toward political modernity with the decapitation of King Charles I in 1649. The 350-year-old English Revolution is a good example of the paradox of modernization. No one would deny the crucial role that England played in the political and economic development of Europe. It was also a country with high levels of literacy early on. But one of the first effects of the English move into modernity was an ideological crisis, expressed politically and religiously, that led to a civil war most Europeans would have a hard time understanding today.

While we may disapprove of their violence, we are able to grasp the general sense of the conflicts that led to the French Revolution, to communist Russia, and to Nazi Germany. The values expressed by these events, whether positive or negative, all seem modern because they are secular. On the other hand, how many Europeans today would be able to choose sides in the metaphysical conflict between Cromwell's Protestant Puritans and the crypto-Catholic partisans of the Stuart kings? In the seventeenth century, it is in the name of God that the English killed each

other, albeit with moderation. I doubt that the English themselves looking back on their history see the military dictatorship
of Cromwell as a necessary stage on the way to the liberal Glorious Revolution of 1688. Pierre Manent got it right when he
placed a pamphlet of the revolutionary poet Milton ("The Freedom to Publish without Permission or Censure," 1644) at the
beginning of his anthology of liberal writings.[5] However, there is
as much religious frenzy as there is defense of liberty in this text,
and another pamphlet by the same author and activist was published five years later to justify the execution of Charles I.

In our own day the Jihad in the name of Allah is not entirely
different in nature from these previous conflicts. Although far
from being always liberal, it is fundamentally not a regression
but, rather, a crisis of transition. The violence and religious
frenzy are only temporary.

The case of Iran is a good example in this respect. In 1979 a religious revolution overthrows the king. This is followed by two
decades of ideological excess and bloody confrontations. But it
was an already high literacy rate that put the Iranian masses into
action in the first place and afterward led the country into a generalized modernization movement. The decline in the birth rate
followed shortly after the rise to power of Ayatollah Khomeini.
The ideological stakes expressed in the Shiite division of Islam are
inaccessible to Europeans of Christian background; however,
they have no less "meaning" than the conflicts between Protestant
sects at the time of Cromwell. The denunciation by Shiite theol-
ogy of the injustice in the world holds a revolutionary potential, as
did the original Protestant metaphysics that perceived man and
society as corrupt. Luther and to an even greater extent Calvin,
those two ayatollahs of the sixteenth century, contributed to the
birth of a regenerated and purified society, namely America, the
progeny of religious exaltation as much as modern-day Iran.

To everyone's surprise, and despite America's refusal to face
the facts, the Iranian revolution is evolving toward a stable set of

democratic practices with elections that, although not exactly free and open, are essentially pluralist with reformers and conservatives, a left and a right.

Although not universal, the three-part process 1) higher literacy, 2) revolution, 3) lower birth rates, is quite common. The basic literacy of men throughout the world advances faster than that of women, with the exception of the Antilles. Political instability instigated by men therefore precedes the spread of control over reproduction that depends essentially on women. In France birth rates began to decrease after the revolution in 1789. In Russia the dramatic decline in the birth rate began after the Bolsheviks gained power and continued through the reign of Stalin.[6]

DEMOGRAPHY AND POLITICS

Higher literacy and lower birth rates, two universal phenomena, make possible the universalization of democracy—something that was observed and intimated more than really explained by Fukuyama, since in his study he was unable to grasp the mental transformation that underlies the march of political history. I know from personal experience that the hypothesis of a correlation between lower birth rates and political modernization can be met with skepticism from political scientists who are not demographers and vice versa. It is so convenient to treat the different dimensions of human history separately and to pretend that the world of politics and the microcosm of the family have nothing to do with each other, as though men and women were all split in two with their two halves each living in separate spheres, either the public life of politics or the private life of reproduction.

In an effort to persuade the reader, allow me to recall how I used the fact of lower birth rates combined with other sets of statistics to predict in *La Chute finale* (1976) the collapse of Soviet communism.[7] The theories that were then fashionable, as well as the thinking of most Sovietologists, accepted the hypothesis formulated most notably by the dissident Alexander Zinoviev of a distinct *Homo Sovieticus* that supposedly was a new type of creature—the product of sixty years of dictatorship and terror. The altered and fixed mental makeup of this *Homo Sovieticus* would in theory allow totalitarianism to go on forever. Trained as I was as both a historian and a demographer, I declared, contrary to conventional thinking, that the lower birth rate in the Soviet Union—42.7 births for one thousand inhabitants in the years 1923–1927, 26.7 for the years 1950–1952, and 18.1 in 1975—would cause perfectly normal Russian citizens to rise up and overthrow communism.[8] In the case of Russia, as with France and Germany, the transition was a particularly unsettled period during which the changes in sexual behavior aggravated the disorientation linked to the rise of literacy. This disorientation corresponds to the Stalinist era.

Even if it is difficult and appears to contradict the evidence, one must understand that the crises and massacres that the media tell us about endlessly are not in most cases simply regressive phenomena, but in fact symptoms of a transitional derailment that is part of the modernization process. One must keep in mind that a stabilizing process will follow automatically and the disturbances will disappear without the least outside intervention.

THE ISLAMIC TRANSITION

If we reexamine the list of areas in the world marked by large-scale violent events at the beginning of the third millennium, one can only be struck by the large number of Muslim countries. Not surprisingly, one notices in recent years the dissemination of the idea that Islam is intrinsically virulent, harmful, and troublesome. Even if China is designated by Huntington as America's principal rival, it is the virulence of Islam and its supposed antagonism with the Christian West that serves as the basis for the arguments put forward in *The Clash of Civilizations*. The roof beams of this roughly hewn work rest on a dubious religious classification. To categorize Russia as Orthodox and China as Confucian can only seem grotesquely silly to anyone familiar with the fundamentally nonreligious lives of Russian and Chinese peasants. In fact, the original failings of religion in these two countries contributed significantly to the success of their communist revolutions that took place in the first half of the twentieth century.

The "theory" of Huntington is essentially the twin of modern Jihad. It is nothing but the mirror image of that of Ayatollah Khomeini who believed, like his shrewd Harvard counterpart, in a conflict of civilizations.

However, it is not necessary to essentialize Islam, point to its supposed taste for war ever since Mahomet's legendary militarism, or denounce the subservience of women in the Arab world to understand the mounting ideological passions and killings within this religious sphere. Although educational levels vary widely in the Muslim world, on the whole it is less developed than Europe, Russia, China, or Japan. This is why one sees at this moment in history a large number of Muslim countries in the process of making the big transition to modernization. They are leaving the less taxing mental routines of an illiterate world and moving toward another type of stability based on universal literacy. Between these two states of equilibrium they encounter the trials and tribulations of being psychologically disoriented.

A few Muslim countries have already accomplished their mental readjustment, a transition that first involved a fundamentalist crisis fueled, as is to be expected, by the younger generation most recently lifted into literacy, with students in the sciences in the front ranks. In Iran this revolution is calming down. In Algeria the extreme Islamism of the Fis (*Front islamique de salut*) has become mired in terrorism and assassinations. In Turkey the increased power of religious parties was unsuccessful in overturning the secular political legacy of Kemal Ataturk. One can only agree with Gilles Kepel, who, in his recent study *Jihad* (2000) describes a worldwide decline of Islamism. With a great deal of historical and sociological precision, Kepel identifies Malaysia—a country where literacy is particularly high (88 percent in 2000)—as the place where the politicoreligious crisis surrounding Islam first started to recede.[9]

One can add the failure of religious militancy in Central Asia to Kepel's overall picture of worldwide Islamic decline. True, there was a civil war in Tajikistan between rival clans some of whom claimed a purist Islamic identity, and Uzbekistan lives in fear of a fundamentalist takeover. However, the fact is that religion plays only a secondary role in the central Asian republics of the former Soviet Union. Many political analysts expected that the fall of communism would provoke an explosion of Islamic religious fervor. But Russia left its former possessions with near-total basic literacy and therefore capable of achieving a rapid demographic transformation between 1975 and 1995. Their political regimes have not broken with some habits acquired during the years of Soviet control. They are certainly far from being true democracies, but they are by no means plagued with religious zealotry.

THE COMING CRISIS: PAKISTAN AND SAUDI ARABIA

Some Muslim countries have only just begun to set out on the road to higher literacy and a modern mindset. The two most important ones in this category are Saudi Arabia (population 35 million in 2001) and Pakistan (population 145 million)—two of the principal actors in the complex scenario that led to the terrorist attacks on the World Trade Center and the Pentagon. The Pakistani army and secret service backed the Taliban regime that provided a base of operations for Al Qaeda, and a majority of the terrorists who took part in the suicide operations against the

United States were of Saudi origin. There is obviously a connec-
tion between the growing hostility toward the United States in
these two countries and their nascent cultural modernization. In
Iran a similar surge in anti-Americanism followed the rise in basic
literacy during the late 1970s. With Iran as a reminder of the experience of going overnight from friend to foe, American leaders are
right to be nervous about the fragility of their strategic position on
both sides of the Persian Gulf. For at least two decades Saudi Arabia and Pakistan will be danger zones where instability could be
expected to increase significantly. Any involvement in these two
regions will include risks, as France learned the hard way when
in May of 2002 a suicide bomber in Karachi exploded a bus carrying technical support staff of the French military.

But one can in no way deduce the existence of universal terrorism from the anti-American feelings of the populations of
these two Muslim countries, both so intimately linked to America's power structure. A large part of the Muslim world is already
in the process of finding a new peaceful equilibrium.

It is too easy to demonize Islam on the basis of recent signs of crisis. Throughout the world Islam is going through its crisis of modernization, and there is no way to disguise the disruptive aspects of
this transition. Developed and more or less orderly countries have
no right to brag about their present state, and were they to meditate
seriously on their own history they might behave with more modesty. The English and French revolutions were violent affairs, and
so were the communist regimes of Russia and China and the military imperialism of Japan. The explicit values associated with the
American War of Independence and the Civil War are immediately comprehensible for the French and others who feel culturally
and historically close to these events. However, the United States
did not escape its own version of the transitional crisis.[10] Certain
ideological debates associated with the American crisis, such as the
fundamental questions surrounding skin color, are difficult for outsiders to understand. To Frenchmen that American idiosyncrasy is

certainly no less strange than the hysterical debates concerning the status of women within Islamic revolutions. ⁊

THE CASE OF YUGOSLAVIA: TWO CRISES COMBINED

The collapse of communism and Yugoslavia, far from disproving the general law associating progress and disorientation, presents particular features that are the result of discrepancies when it comes to educational, demographic, and economic development among the various populations that together constituted the former Yugoslav federation.[11] The demographic transitions among Serbs, Croatians, and Slovenians did not happen as early as those in Western Europe, but they were more or less complete by 1955. The birth rate at that time was 2.5 in Croatia and Slovenia, and 2.8 in Serbia. In these republics the rise in literacy led to lower birth rates and to the spread of communist ideology. Further south, in Bosnia, Kosovo, Macedonia, and Albania, communism was forced on societies that had not yet fully reached the stage of modern thinking and education. In 1966 the birth rate in Bosnia was still 4.3, in Macedonia 4.7, and in Albania and Kosovo 6.7. The moderately high numbers for Bosnia and Macedonia reflect the religious diversity within these republics: Catholics, Orthodox Christians, and Muslims in the case of Bosnia, and Orthodox Christians and Muslims in Kosovo and Macedonia. Without considering the religious classifications as anything more than a set of labels that permit one to identify different cultural systems, one can see that the Muslim populations in the region are clearly out of sync and lagging behind the Christian populations in their movement toward modernity. These mixed southern entities nevertheless obey the general law of transition. By 1975 Bosnia's birth rate had fallen to 2.3, Macedonia reached the same level in 1984, and Kosovo in 1998. Albania was close behind these three, having reached a birth rate of 2.5 in 1998.

With the help of demographic analysis, one can identity two crises of transition toward modernity within the territory encompassed by the former Yugoslavia and Albania. The first crisis extended from 1930 to 1955 and led the "Christian" populations, mostly Croatians and Serbs, toward mental and demographic modernization through communism. The second crisis, which we can date from 1965 to 2000, led the Islamized populations toward the same modernity. However, what ought to be called the belated revolution in thinking within the Muslim communities interfered with the fall of communism, something that should have served the Serbs and Croatians as a sort of phase 2 conclusion to their crisis of modernization. But with all of these populations mixed together, it is clear now that the end of communism — technically complex in itself — was transformed by the transitional crisis of the Muslim populations into a murderous nightmare.

The fact that the first outbreaks of violence concerned Serbs and Croatians does not mean that the "Muslim question" did not exist from the beginning of the crisis. One must keep in mind that the variable degree and extent of demographic transformation had the effect of creating constant modifications in the relative weight of this or that group, and this in turn created on the federal level a general anxiety about who would maintain control over what territory and how. Having moved toward lower birth rates earlier than others, the Serbs and Croatians experienced slower growth and watched apprehensively the rapid growth of the Muslim population, something they perceived as a threatening demographic invasion. The ethnic obsessions of the post-communist era were exacerbated by these differing demographic dynamics. They came to the surface amidst the problematic separation of Croatians from Serbs.

We are here in a realm of ideology and speculation that does not permit any scientific verification as such. However, it is doubtful that the ethnic cleansing between Serbs and Croatians would have risen to the levels it did without the Muslim catalyst—that is, a rapidly expanding minority population that was going through its own crisis of modernization. In contrast, the independence movement of the Slovenians, situated to the north and thus far from any Muslim influence, provoked hardly any more distress than the separation of Czechs from Slovaks in the territory of the former Czechoslovakia.

The purpose of such a "technical" analysis is not to claim that all humanitarian aid is pointless. When the countries involved are small, one can imagine that outside help could serve to lower tensions. An effort at greater historical and sociological understanding, however, ought to precede the intervention by military powers that are themselves far removed from the painful challenges of modernization. The Yugoslavian crisis gave rise to a great deal of moral posturing but unfortunately little substantive analysis. Anyone looking at a map of the world could easily notice, stretching from Yugoslavia to Central Asia, a broad zone of ideological interaction—not between Islam and Christianity, as Huntington would have us believe, but between Islam and communism. The accidental conjunction of the Islamic transition and the decline of communism, in effect the simultaneous unfolding of two phases, early and late, of modernization, was a frequent occurrence in the 1990s and would have merited a general sociological study. The major conflicts in the Caucasus region and the smaller ones in Central Asia show many similarities to the Yugoslavian confrontations. The basic point is that the superposition of two transitional crises renders the accomplishment of each more difficult, but it does not imply a permanent or structural state of conflict between populations.

THE NEED FOR PATIENCE AND LONGER VIEWS

Generally, higher literacy and lower birth rates are only achieved at the cost of ideological and political upheaval between opposing classes, religions, and ethnicities. A few countries have managed to avoid civil war and genocide, although not without some version of transitional anxiety all the same. And yet I would hesitate to name any particular country for fear that I may be forgetting about some past crisis or massacre. Perhaps the Scandinavian countries escaped the worst if one thinks of Denmark, Sweden, or Norway. Linguistically complex Finland, on the other hand, experienced a civil war between Reds and Whites in the aftermath of the First World War and in the wake of the Russian Revolution.

If one goes back to the origins of the Protestant Reformation when literacy really takes off, we find the feverish Swiss, shaken by religious passion and perfectly capable of butchering each other over grand ideas and burning heretics and witches—all this on the way to acquiring their legendary reputation for cleanliness and punctuality and eventually becoming the headquarters of the Red Cross and a center for the dissemination of lessons on civil harmony throughout the world. Therefore, out of simple decency, we ought to refrain from making categorical claims about Islam being different by nature and stop making pat judgments about its presumed "essence."

Unfortunately, the events of September 11, 2001, have increased the circulation of the idea of a "clash of civilizations." In most cases, perhaps under the pressure to seem "tolerant" in today's politically correct spheres, the phrase circulated with a tinge of Br'er Rabbit double-talk. The suspiciously large number of commentators and politicians who vocally claimed in the days, weeks, and months following the terrorist attacks that 911 *in no way constituted a "clash of civilizations" between Islam and Christianity* strongly suggests that this primitive idea was on everybody's mind. The polite talk that has now worked its way into the speech habits of the 20 percent who make up the new overclass forbids making direct accusations against Islam. But Islamic fundamentalism has become a code word for a "terrorism" that many wish to believe is universal.

In point of fact, as we have tried to show, September 11 occurred after the Islamic fever had already begun to subside. Higher literacy and lower birth rates permit one to track and explain in depth the leveling off of the Islamic ideological curve. This analysis also allows one to say that the United States and any of its allies who want to venture into the briar patch of Saudi Arabia or Pakistan should be forewarned about the difficulties of meddling with countries that are preparing for the big leap into modernity with all the convulsions that usually accompany this experience. Lately the United States has used the notion of universal terrorism to redefine itself as the leader of a worldwide "crusade" and to justify interventions anywhere at any time and for any length of time—short, as in the Philippines and Yemen, or long, as in the case of the military bases in Afghanistan and Uzbekistan and its strategic deployments on Georgia's border with Chechnya. However, no historical or sociological justification of such a notion is possible for anyone willing to examine the facts of the real world. "Universal terrorism" is absurd from the standpoint of the Muslim world, which will eventually work its way through its transitional crisis without outside intervention. It could only be useful to the United States if it somehow needs to have an Old World embroiled in a state of permanent war.

2

Democracy as a Threat

Studying the effects of education and demographics adds some substance to Fukuyama's hypothesis concerning the direction of history. Today, literacy and control over reproduction appear to be universal human drives. Furthermore, it is easy to see that these two features of human progress are linked to a rise in "individualism" and the affirmation of the individual within the political sphere. Aristotle offered one of the first definitions of democracy when he anticipated the modern association between freedom (*eleutheria*) and equality (*isonomia*) as the key to allowing man to "live as he likes" (*Politics* 1310,a32).[1]

Learning to read and write brings each person to a higher level of consciousness. The fall of birth rates is a prime symptom of these deep psychological changes. Thus, given the universal tendency toward complete literacy and demographic equilibrium, it is not illogical to witness a rapid proliferation of more democratic political regimes. One could advance the hypothesis that individuals who have been made conscious and free through literacy cannot be governed indefinitely in authoritarian ways; or, what amounts to the same thing, the practical costs of exerting authoritarian rule over a critically aware population renders the society in which they live economically uncompetitive. Indeed, there is much to say about the relationship between education and democracy. This association was perfectly clear to men such as Condorcet, who placed progress in education at the center of his *Esquisse d'un tableau historique des progrès de l'esprit humain.*[2] Although De Tocqueville did not have education in mind when he spoke of the "providential" march of democracy, this was the underlying historical factor.[3]

This scenario seems to me more genuinely "Hegelian" than Fukuyama's proposal, which gets bogged down in economic determinism and obsessions over material progress. It also seems to me to be more realistic and probable as an explanation of the multiplication of democracies in Eastern Europe, the former Soviet republics, Latin America, Turkey, Iran, Indonesia, Taiwan, and Korea. One can hardly explain the spread of pluralist electoral systems by pointing to the growing prosperity of the world. The era of globalization has been marked by lower economic growth rates, slower increases and sometimes declines in the standard of living of the average citizen, and almost always greater inequality. It is hard to believe in economic explanations: How could growing material uncertainty lead to the overthrow of dictatorial regimes and the establishment of free and open electoral procedures? Progress in education, on the other hand, allows one to grasp how one could have greater intellectual equality while still maintaining economic inequality.

No matter what one might say against Fukuyama, it is not unreasonable to entertain his hypothesis of a world one day unified by liberal democracy, with the added bonus of a generalized peace following from the Doyle law that claims it is impossible for two democracies to go to war against each other. We must keep in mind, however, that the paths being taken by the different countries and regions of the world are quite diverse.

Common sense alone makes one doubt whether an absolute convergence around one liberal economic and political model is possible among nations that have had such different historical experiences as the French revolution, communism, Nazism, fascism, Khomeinism, Vietnamese national communism, and Cambodia's Khmer Rouge. Fukuyama raises his own doubts about the reality of such a convergence when he discusses the present Japanese democracy, which appears perfect from the outside but has the peculiarity of having maintained the liberal-democratic party in power since 1945 except for the brief interregnum of less than one year over parts of 1993 and 1994. In Japan the choice of governments is the result of battles between clans within the dominant party. For Fukuyama the absence of any rotation of the party in power does not disqualify Japan from being considered a democracy because it is the result of the free choice of the voters.

The Swedish government that has for so long been dominated by the Social Democratic party has certain similarities with the Japanese model. To the extent that the Swedish system is an endogenous creation with no foreign occupation at its start as is the case with Japan, one can perhaps accept Fukuyama's definition of liberal democracy that does not see the rotation of power as a necessary condition.

Taken together the alternation of parties in the Anglo-Saxon world and the continuity within the Japanese and Swedish systems suggest that there are distinct subspecies of democracy and that therefore a complete global convergence is unlikely.

SOME ANTHROPOLOGICAL SYSTEMS

The fundamental problem that orthodox political science runs up against today is that it has no convincing explanation for the dramatic ideological diversity among societies going through their phase of modernization. We saw in the previous chapter what all of these examples of cultural development have in common: higher literacy, lower birth rates, political activation of the masses, and the temporary disarray and violence that results from mental deracination. One must concede, however, that the military dictatorship of Cromwell that authorized the sharing of churches between rival Protestant sects on the one hand, and the Bolshevik dictatorship that established concentration camps over an entire continent on the other were each expressing different values. It is also true that while communist totalitarianism was strongly attached to the principle of equality among men, Nazi ideology made the inequality of peoples a prime article of faith.

In *La Troisième planète: Structures familiales et systèmes idéologiques* (1983), I put forward an anthropological explanation for the political divergence of societies going through modernization.[4] A kinship-based theory would allow one to describe and understand the persistent diversity within the democratic world that may be coming into existence.

The family systems of peasants uprooted by modernization transmitted diverse sets of values—liberal or authoritarian, egalitarian or unegalitarian—that were reincorporated within the ideological constructions of the modern world.

Anglo-Saxon liberalism transfers into the political sphere the idea of mutual independence between parents and children that characterises the English family as well as the absence of an egalitarian obligation between brothers.

The French revolution makes a universal doctrine of the liberty and equality of man out of the liberalism characteristic of the relations between parents and children and the equality among brothers that one finds in northern France in the eighteenth century.

The Russian Muzhiks treated their sons equally but kept them under parental authority all their lives, whether married or bachelors. The Russian transitional ideology of communism, therefore, was not just egalitarian as in France but also authoritarian. This model was adopted in all areas where family structures of the Russian type predominated such as in China, Yugoslavia, and Vietnam, as well as among the peasants of certain communist-voting pockets of Europe such as in Tuscany, the Limoges area of central France, and Finland.

The authoritarian and unegalitarian ideology of the Nazi party that came to power in Germany was consistent with the authoritarian and unegalitarian values of the traditional German family that designated within each generation a single inheritor. Japan and Sweden can be considered as attenuated versions of this anthropological type.

Arab family structures allow one to explain certain aspects of radical Islamism, a transitional ideology among others, but one that is characterized by the singular aspiration to combine egalitarianism with a specific conception of community that has difficulty establishing a strong state. This particular anthropological type exists outside the Arab world in places such as Iran, Pakistan, Afghanistan, Uzbekistan, Tajikistan, Kyrgyzstan, Azerbaijan, and a part of Turkey. The very low status of women within this anthropological type is only its most obvious characteristic. It shares with the Russian family model a communitarian organization that links fathers and married sons; however, it is quite distinct in its preference for endogamous marriage between cousins. Marriages between first cousins, particularly between the children of two brothers, lead to very specific relations of authority both within the family and within the larger ideology that builds on this family pattern. The father-son relationship is not truly authoritarian. The custom overshadows the father, and it is the horizontal association between brothers that really counts. This system is very egalitarian and communitarian; however, it is hardly one that fosters respect for authority, and state authority in particular.[5] The level of endogamy varies by region: 15 percent in Turkey, 25–30 percent in the Arab world, and 50 percent in Pakistan. From an anthropological point of view, I am rather curious to see how Pakistan will go about its psychological and ideological transition to modernity given the country's extreme position when it comes to endogamy. One can be sure already that its modernization will be different from that of Iran, for example, where the level of endogamy is only 25 percent. Pakistan's status as an American ally has already come into question, and the future manifestations of its particular transitional ideology will most likely cause other surprises.

It would be possible to give other examples and outline the specific developmental challenges of each. The important thing to acknowledge here is that prior to the process of modernization there is an initial anthropological system defined by the geography and customs of the peasant population. Whole regions and peoples that are carriers of diverse sets of family values are led in suc-

TABLE 3. Percent of Marriages Between First
Cousins During the Years 1990–1995

Sudan	57
Pakistan	50
Mauritania	40
Tunisia	36
Jordan	36
Saudi Arabia	36
Syria	35
Oman	33
Yemen	31
Qatar	30
Kuwait	30
Algeria	29
Egypt	25
Morocco	25
United Arab Emirates	25
Iran	25
Bahrain	23
Turkey	15

SOURCE: *Demographic and Health Survey*

cession and more or less rapidly through the same movement of deracination. If we take into account, on the one hand, the diversity of traditional family customs in the original peasant world—the anthropological variable—and on the other hand, the universal advance of literacy—the historical variable—we can grasp simultaneously the unique direction of history and the diversity of particular phenomena.

ONE POSSIBLE SCENARIO: HYSTERICAL TRANSITIONS FOLLOWED BY DEMOCRATIC CONVERGENCE

In a first stage the transitional crisis accentuates the anthropological values. As a reaction formation to the disorientation caused by modernity, one witnesses a hardened ideological affirmation of the traditional family values. This is why transitional ideologies are all more or less fundamentalist and purist. Consciously or not, they all assert their attachment to the past, even when they pretend to be resolutely modern, as in the case of communism, for example. The single party, the centralized economy, and most of all the KGB all reproduced at the level of the Russian state the totalitarian role of the traditional peasant family.[6]

All traditional societies are being pulled by the same historical movement: literacy. However, the various transitions dramatize the differences between peoples and nations. Thus the antagonisms between, say, French and Germans or between English and Russians appear extremely high because each group is barking, as it were, under the ideological tree that issued from its own original anthropological roots. Today, the Muslim-Arab world is dramatizing one last time its differences with the West, notably over the status of women, while at the same time the women of Iran and others throughout the Arab world are in the process of emancipating themselves through contraception.

Then the crisis subsides. It gradually becomes clear that all the anthropological types are being reshaped, at different speeds but nevertheless in parallel, by the same rise in individualism that comes with literacy. Signs of a convergence toward democracy eventually emerge.

Of course, all the different types of anthropological system do not confront the rise in democratic individualism in the same way. How could they? The value of liberty is for certain systems, notably the French and Anglo-Saxon models, inscribed within the original family pattern; the movement of history only formalizes and makes more explicit what was already there. On the other hand, the same strengthening of individualism attacks certain traditional anthropological values that lie deep within the German, Japanese, Russian, Chinese, and Arab systems—hence the greater amounts of violence associated with their transitional processes and certain differences in their outcomes. For example, the original values of authority and community that characterize these systems become attenuated but are not altogether eliminated. We are thus able to take account of observable differences between various types of democracy coexisting peacefully in the world after the demographic transition. Japan, with its unbeatable liberal-democratic party, its social cohesion, and its industrialized and export-based capitalism, is clearly not the United States. Nor will postcommunist Russia and post-Khomeini Iran adopt the hyper-individualized social forms that predominate in America.

It is difficult to accept the idea that all of the "democracies" emerging or likely to emerge from the various transitional crises will be essentially stable, or that they will be similar in their modes of functioning to the liberal Anglo-Saxon and French democracies. To contemplate the possibility of a peaceful world, to acknowledge a general tendency toward greater individualism, and to believe in the universal triumph of liberal democracy are, however, quite different things. But for now at any rate, there is no reason to be contemptuous toward the Fukuyama hypothesis.

Even the failure of the first postcommunist democratic exper-
iment in China that led to a mixed regime combining economic
liberalism with political authoritarianism does not necessarily
overturn Fukuyama's theory. One can understand this as a provi-
sional phase within the transition. The example of Taiwan, where
over the last few years one can observe the development of true
democracy, proves that there is no fundamental incompatibility
between democracy and China, the skeptical theses of Huntington notwithstanding.

It is much more difficult to imagine a future stabilization of
democratic and liberal institutions in Latin America with its broken up rather than individualistic family units, its radically unegalitarian economic structures, and wracked as it has been by
alternating cycles of democratization and military putsches since
the nineteenth century. In fact, even a sustained authoritarian
stabilization is difficult to imagine in the case of Latin America
for anyone who knows its history. And yet, despite formidable
economic difficulties and political twists and turns that are hard
to describe, democracy in Argentina is still standing. In
Venezuela, where the business leaders, the church, private television stations, and a part of the army attempted a coup d'état
against President Hugo Chavez in April 2002, democracy exhib-
ited an unexpected hardiness. We must remember that the literacy rate among adults today is 93 percent and 98 percent among
young Venezualans aged fifteen to twenty-four. A few television
stations are not enough to brainwash a population that knows
how to read and not just watch. The changes in thinking are profound if one takes birth control as a yardstick. The Venezuelan
birth rate fell to an average of 2.9 at the beginning of 2002.

The resilience of the Venezuelan democracy has been particularly surprising to American leaders, who rushed to approve of
the coup, an interesting sign of a new indifference to principles
of a liberal democracy. One can imagine Fukuyama was thrilled
to see the democratic resistance of Venezuela that further con-

firms his hypothesis; but he might be troubled to see the United States officially turn its back on the principles of liberty and equality at the very moment when they are triumphing in the former "Third World."

If we keep to the limited designs of this book, which aims to examine the realignment of America's relations with the rest of the world, it is not necessary to give a definitive answer to the question of the general democratization of the planet. It is enough to observe that after a distinct phase of modernization, societies are quieting down and finding forms of nontotalitarian government that are acceptable to a majority of the population. It is enough, in other words, to accept a minimum version of Fukuyama's hypothesis about the universalization of liberal democracy. The same minimalist approach can be used with regard to the Doyle law concerning the impossibility of war between democracies. One might prudently formulate a more general and less dogmatic hypothesis that would claim war was not likely to break out between these newly tranquil societies. To decide whether the recent democratization of these political systems—fueled by the movement toward universal literacy—will one day make them into strict equivalents of the liberal French and Anglo-Saxon models is of secondary importance.

THE UNITED NATIONS OF EUROPE

The territory of Western Europe is certainly the most suitable area of application for the thought experiments derived from the work of Fukuyama and Doyle even if its inability to attain its equilibrium unassisted prevents it from being an absolutely convincing example. The United States militarily enforced the establishment and stabilization of liberal democracy in Western Europe after the end of World War II. West Germany was for a number of years, like Japan, a kind of American protectorate. All the same, after two centuries of excessive ideological and physical warfare, the transformation of Europe into a peaceful zone of cooperation between all nations illustrates the potential for a peaceful world. At the center of Europe, the friendly relations between France and Germany are an especially important example of a long-time war zone transforming itself into something that strongly resembles a region of perpetual peace.[7]

The democratic and peaceful equilibrium that is establishing itself in Europe does not at all mean that there has been a total convergence toward a single sociopolitical model. The old nation-states with their languages, social structures, and customs are still very much alive. To demonstrate their persistence, we could examine the diversity of methods for dealing with conflicts, the systems of political parties, and the types of alternation of the ruling party. However, we can also take a look at the fundamental reality on the level of demographics.

When it comes to birth rates, all the European nations have completed their modernizing transition. The averages, however, vary widely, from 1.1 to 1.9 births per woman. If one considers the large nations of Europe—that appear medium or small on the scale of the world taken as a whole—it is possible to correlate birth rates with ideological traditions. Great Britain and France are remarkable for having birth rates that are reasonably high, 1.7 and 1.9, respectively. These numbers are close to the 2.1 rate of zero growth and to the 1.8 births per woman that is the average for the white population of European origin in the United States.[7] The three oldest liberal democracies remain close in this regard. Elsewhere, birth rates have collapsed: 1.3 in Germany and Italy, 1.2 in Spain—three countries that experienced dictatorships as part of their transitional phase in the first half of the twentieth century. These differences are perhaps not accidental. With the arrival of modern methods of contraception—pill, IUD, diaphragm—couples have fallen into an oddly natural state of infertility. Whereas it used to be necessary to fight against nature and *decide* not to have too many children, today it is necessary to *decide* to have one or more children. Populations with traditions of individualism such as the United States, France, and Great Britain seem to have less trouble with this change of perspective. However, among populations living in areas that are traditionally more authoritarian, one notices, on the demographic level, a more passive idea of human existence. In these places, the decision regarding fertility, which has now become a proactive one, is more difficult to make.

Such an explanation would imply that profound differences in ways of thinking persist among European populations, and notably between France and Germany. This difference in temperament, however, does not prevent either government from respecting the rules of democracy even if the ruling party in Germany does not change very frequently while in France it is rare for any political side to win more than two elections in a row.

Given the singular existence of each European nation—if one looks beyond their shared institutions, common currency, and technological collaboration—it would be more accurate, and perhaps more inspiring, to speak of the United Nations of Europe.

Let us return now to the global picture and look at things from the standpoint of history in general with only our common sense to guide us and no obstacles such as philosophical references or reassuring political theories in our way. How can one not see that a completely literate world that has reached demographic equilibrium would have a tendency toward peace that would extend the recent history of Europe over the entire globe? We can indeed imagine peaceful nations devoted to their spiritual and material development. We can also imagine the world following the path already taken by the United States, Western Europe, and Japan since the end of the Second World War—a path that would lead to the triumph of the doctrine of the "United Nations."

This world is perhaps a dream. However, it is certain that were it to come into existence, it would model its political form on that of the existing United Nations Organization without any special role accorded to the United States. The United States would have to become just one liberal democracy among others, scale back its military machine, retire from its geostrategic activities, and humbly accept the gratitude of the rest of the planet for its long years of exemplary service.

This page of history is unlikely to be written. We do not yet know if the universalization of liberal democracy and peace is an inevitable historical process. We do know, however, that such a world poses a threat to the United States. Economically dependent, America requires a minimum level of global disorder in order to justify its politicomilitary presence in the Old World.

A RETURN TO STRATEGIC REALISM: RUSSIA AND PEACE

Let us conclude by going back to where we began and consider the country whose first steps toward democratization were the inspiration for Fukuyama's hypothetical vision in the first place: Russia. Just before the ideological collapse of the Soviet Union, this gigantic country in terms of landmass, population, and military sophistication was a potential threat to every other country on the planet. The military expansionism of the Soviet Union was the fundamental problem for the Western democracies and alone justified the role of the United States as protector of the free world. The fall of communism might allow for the establishment of a liberal democracy in Russia in the near future. If a liberal democracy cannot, by its nature, attack another liberal democracy, the changes in Russia's political life would be sufficient to transform the whole planet into a peaceful sphere. Once Russia becomes a harmless giant, Europeans and the Japanese will no longer need the United States as protector. For the United States this would be a painful new scenario since it relies heavily on the industrial and financial resources of Europe and Japan.

We may speculate further. If the Old World evolves toward peace, if it no longer needs the United States, and if, on the other hand, the United States becomes economically voracious and threatening, then the role of Russia might also reverse itself. There is nothing to prevent one from imagining that a liberal and democratic Russia might one day protect the planet from America's aggressive attempts to regain its global imperial status.

I will examine in detail the economic situation and the strategic role of Russia in a later chapter. For now we need only recall that Russia's nuclear arsenal, despite the erosion in other areas of its military, makes it the only country that stands in the way of America's complete military dominance. The agreement of May 2002 between George W. Bush and Vladimir Putin concerning reductions in their nuclear arsenals left over two thousand nuclear warheads on either side and therefore does little to efface the old Cold War atmosphere of mutual terror.

If the relationship of America to the rest the world is turning upside down as the former changes from protector into potential aggressor, the relationship of Russia to the rest of the world must also turn upside down, going from aggressor to potential protector. Ultimately, the only stable element, according to this model, would be the antagonistic character of Russian-American relations.

3

Imperial Dimensions

Anyone who wants to think about the American order against the general background of history will want to reflect on the ancient empires of Greece and Rome. The former is often invoked by those sympathetic to the United States, the latter by anti-Americans. A favorable attitude toward what goes on in Washington generally leads to comparisons with Athens. It is noted, for example, that in the case of the United States, the establishment of a sphere of political domination beyond its national borders has not been the result of a military conquest as was the case with the Roman Empire.

Roman history is the history of the acquisition of territory. The genetic code of that city-state seems to have included the principle of expansion by force of arms. Everything else—internal politics, economics, art—was secondary. Athens, on the other hand, started out as a city of traders and artisans, the birthplace of Greek tragedy, philosophy, and democracy. It was forced to take military action to defend itself against Persian aggression, and with Sparta it became one of the two cities of Greek resistance. After a first Persian defeat, Sparta, a landlocked city, withdrew from the conflict, while Athens, a naval power, went on to organize a confederation of cities known as the Delian League.[1] The most powerful furnished ships; the weakest offered money. By means of this type of democratic leadership an Athenian sphere of influence was first established.

The United States started out as essentially a naval power like Athens. Moreover, the country was decidedly isolationist up until Pearl Harbor and could hardly be accused of congenital militarism and territorial imperialism in the Roman style. The NATO constitution was enthusiastically ratified by the European allies of the United States. Drawing a parallel between the North Atlantic Treaty Organization and the Delian League is not far-fetched, and one could extend the analogy by casting the Soviet Union in the role of the Persian aggressor.

However, only those who have forgotten subsequent episodes of Athenian history could possibly be seduced by this optimistic and liberal vision of NATO. The Delian League degenerated rather quickly. The majority of the allied cities preferred to meet their military obligations by paying tribute (*phoros*) to Athens instead of furnishing ships or sailors. The ruling city ended up appropriating for itself the common wealth that was kept on the island of Delos and used it to finance the subjugation of the recalcitrant cities of the League and also the temples of the Acropolis. The example is imperfect, or too perfect: it could lead Europeans—and why not the Japanese?—to conduct a "realist" meditation on their own military behavior.

Athens was finally defeated by Sparta, the city that, as the wheel of fortune turned, found itself transformed into the defender of Greek freedom. Unfortunately, the historical records that have survived do not allow us to analyze with precision the economic advantages that Athens derived from its empire nor the effect that these profits had on the social structure of the city itself.[2]

POLITICAL AND MILITARY ORIGINS OF
ECONOMIC GLOBALIZATION

The considerably larger number of people who claim the proper analogy is between the United States and the Roman Empire like to point out that the history of the American empire did not begin in 1948 in response to the coup in Prague and in general as a reaction to the establishment of the Soviet sphere of influence. They contend that the American system was established in 1945 at the end of a world war during which the United States had affirmed its industrial and military supremacy. The fundamental conquests of the new American order that began in 1945 were the protectorates of Germany and Japan, two considerable additions given their economic importance. Germany was the world's second largest industrial power before the war, and Japan is the second largest today. It is clearly by military force that the United States established its ascendancy over these two states, the two foci essential for control over the world economy. This is what makes one think of the Roman Empire when contemplating U.S. history.

The case of Rome is better documented than that of Athens when it comes to economic and social dimensions. It is possible to measure the distortion of the Roman social order caused by the accumulation in the capital of wealth produced in the outer regions that were all under military domination.

For one hundred years following its decisive victory over Carthage, at the end of the second Punic War, Rome expanded rapidly toward the east and became master over the entire Mediterranean Basin. It then had unlimited resources in terms of land, money, and slaves. It collected taxes or tribute throughout its empire and was able to transfer to the central capital massive quantities of foodstuffs and manufactured items. The peasants and the artisans of Italy saw their economic base disappear as this Mediterranean economy was "globalized" by the political domination of

Rome. The society was polarized between, on the one hand, a mass of economically useless plebeians and, on the other, a predatory plutocracy. A minority gorged with wealth oversaw the remaining proletarianized population. The middle classes collapsed, a process that brought about the end of the republic and the beginning of the political form known as "empire" in conformity with the observations made by Aristotle (*Politics* 4.11) about the importance of intermediate social classes for the stability of political systems.[3]

Since one could not eliminate the plebeians, intractable but geographically central as they were, they came to be nourished and distracted at the empire's expense with "bread and circuses."[4]

For anyone who is interested in today's American-led economic globalization, the comparison with these ancient models is highly instructive both for the resemblances as well as the differences. Whether one insists on the Athenian or the Roman precedent, it is evident that the economic domination of a particular sphere has political and military origins. This political vision of economics corrects, in the optician's sense of the term, the popular view that sees globalization as an apolitical phenomenon. According to this reigning dogma, there is such a thing as a liberal economic world in which nations, states, and military powers do not exist. However, if one keeps in mind the Athenian and Roman examples, it is impossible not to see that the establishment of a globalized world economy is the result of a politicomilitary process and that certain odd features of the globalized economy cannot be explained without referring to the politicomilitary dimension of the system.

FROM PRODUCTION TO CONSUMPTION

Liberal economic theory has a great deal to say when it comes to singing the praises of free trade as the only principle capable of optimizing production and consumption for all inhabitants of the planet. It insists on the necessity that each country should specialize in the production of the kinds of goods and services for which it is most suited or talented. It then speculates endlessly about the automatic, self-regulating nature of market changes: large and magnificent equilibria establish themselves between production versus consumption and imports versus exports, thanks to the mediating fluctuations in exchange rates between national currencies. Textbook economics perceives, describes, or invents—as the case may be—an ideal, perfectly symmetrical world in which the status of all nations is equivalent and all work for the common good. This theory, which germinated in the writings of Smith and Ricardo, has grown into the dominant economic culture produced and reproduced on most major American university campuses today. It is, along with music and movies, one of the leading cultural exports of the United States. It is also about as faithful to reality as a major motion picture from Hollywood. This theory has less to say, and can even lose its voice entirely, when it comes to explaining the troubling fact that globalization is not organized around a principle of symmetry but of asymmetry. Increasingly, the rest of the world is producing so that America can consume. There is no equilibrium between exports and imports establishing itself where the United States is concerned. This nation that was so autonomous and overproductive immediately after World War II has become the center of a system in which its number one job is to consume rather than to produce.

The list of American trade deficits country by country is impressive because it includes all the important nations of the world. For the year 2001, America's trade deficit with China was 83 billion dollars, with Japan 68 billion; 60 billion with the combined European Union, of which 29 billion was Germany's share, Italy's 13 billion, and France's 10 billion. The U.S. trade deficit with Mexico in 2001 was 30 billion, with South Korea 13 billion. Even Israel, Russia, and Ukraine have positive trade balances with the U.S. to the tune of 4.5, 3.5, and 0.5 billion dollars, respectively.

As one can perhaps tell from this list of countries with a positive trade balance vis-à-vis the United States, the importation of natural resources is not the main cause of the American deficit, a situation that would be quite normal for a developed country. For example, oil, the American strategic obsession, only accounts for 80 billion dollars within the 2001 trade deficit; the rest, essentially manufactured goods, represents 366 billion.

If we correlate the American deficit not with the global GNP that includes agriculture and services but simply with the total value of industrial production, we come to the stupefying realization that 10 percent of America's industrial consumption depends on imported goods for which there is no corresponding balance in national exports. This industrial deficit has doubled in little over five years since it stood at 5 percent in 1995. Low technology items are not the staple of these "extra" imported goods, although American industry remains the leader in a number of areas, notably computers, medical products, and aeronautics. Nevertheless, year after year the American lead is shrinking in all areas, including these three. In 2003 Airbus will build as many planes as Boeing even though Toulouse will not pull even with the Seattle giant in terms of total value until 2005–2006. The positive American trade balance, when only "advanced technology" is counted, dropped from 35 billion dollars in 1990 to 5 billion in 2001 and had disappeared entirely to become one more element in the overall trade deficit in January 2002.[5]

The speed with which the American industrial deficit has appeared is one of the most interesting aspects of the current process. On the eve of the Great Depression of 1929, 44.5 percent of global industrial production was based in the United States as opposed to 11.6 percent in Germany, 9.3 percent in Great Britain, 7 percent in France, 4.6 percent in the Soviet Union, 3.2 percent in Italy, and 2.4 percent in Japan.[6] Seventy years later the industrial production of the United States is lower than the combined production of the European Union and only slightly higher than that of Japan.

This fall in economic strength is not compensated for by the activities of American-based multinationals. Since 1998 the profits that they bring back into the country amount to less than what foreign companies that have set up shop in theUnited States are taking back to their own countries.

THE NECESSITY OF A COPERNICAN REVOLUTION:
GOODBYE TO "INTERNAL" STATISTICS

Before the recession of 2001 most economic experts were celebrating the fantastic dynamism of the American economy with its creation of a new paradigm combining the power of investment, vigorous consumption, low unemployment, and low inflation. The 1970s challenge of how to square the circle had finally been solved—America had discovered how to have steady growth without excessively rising prices. By the start of 2002 worrying about the lagging production of Europe and Japan had become a standard refrain of the European media. But at the same time the U.S. government was preparing to reinstate higher tariffs to defend its outmoded steel industry, sales of the Japanese video consoles Play Station II and Game Cube had far out-paced X-Box—Microsoft's attempt to compete in this lucrative market; California was experiencing blackouts due to an electricity and taxation imbroglio; and New York was having trouble with its supply of drinking water.

As early as five years ago the glowing accounts of the American economy and the real significance of growth rates of GNP that seemed mysterious at best all struck me as rather suspicious. Increasingly, we are confronted with a choice: one can either believe the GNP statistics that are based on the total value of business activities within the United States, or else one can rely on the picture one gets from examining the trade balance. The latter, a measure of trade between countries, reveals that the

United States is industrially weak. When the importation of a product proves difficult, tensions can spread fast as we saw with the electricity shortage in California that resulted in last year's blackouts.

I have long wondered about the reality of America's alleged economic dynamism. Since the Enron and Arthur Andersen scandals things have become clear. The bankruptcy of Enron, an energy brokerage company, involved the disappearance of 100 billion dollars in sales—or at least this was the magical, mythical, virtual number cited in the press. The accounting fraud practiced by their auditor, Arthur Andersen, makes it impossible to say today what percentage of that sum was the "value added" portion that ought to have been added in to come up with America's GNP figures. Still, to get a statistical "feeling" one must keep in mind that 100 billion dollars represents roughly 1 percent of America's GNP. How many companies with the help of Andersen or other such accounting firms are falsifying their business statements? The growing number of accounting scandals in recent months suggests that the majority of them are concerned in some way. What kind of economy is this where financial services, insurers, and the real estate market have grown twice as fast as industry from 1994 to 2000, such that today the "value" of their production is equal to 123 percent of industry? I put the word *value* in quotation marks since the value of these services as opposed to that of industrial goods is that the former cannot be exchanged on international markets. Swollen by all the fraudulent practices of private companies, the American GNP is starting to resemble that of the former Soviet Union when it comes to trusting the numbers.

Orthodox economic theory cannot explain the shrinking of American industrial activity nor the transformation of the United States into a country whose specialty is consumption and one that relies on foreign imports to carry out that role. However, an imperial model of the Roman type does allow one to understand this

TABLE 4. Economic Sectors and Their Growth Rates in the United States

	Fraction of Gross Domestic Product (GDP) in 2000	Growth 1994–2000
Gross Domestic Product (GDP)	100	40
Agriculture	1.4	15
Mining	1.3	41
Construction	4.7	68
Manufacturing	15.9	28
Transportation	8.4	35
Wholesale Trade	6.8	41
Retail Trade	9.1	44
Finance, Insurance, Real Estate	19.6	54
Services	21.9	59
Government	12.3	27

SOURCE: *Bureau of Economic Analysis*; http://www.bea.gov/dn2/gpoc.htm#1994–2000

process, namely as the economic consequences of a specific political and military organization.

At the end of the Second World War, faced as it was with the devastation of Europe and Japan and the increasing strength of the Soviet system, the United States transformed its specific sphere of influence into a global system with itself at the center. Step by step, rules of the game that corresponded to the ideological preferences of the United States were adopted in the areas of commerce and finance so as to reinforce the military and political control over this area. There is no question that early on the American claim to insure the well-being of most of the planet was perfectly justified. It would be absurd to consider the emergence of this global system as at base a destructive phenomenon—the growth of the years 1950–1975 proves it. The Marshall Plan, which gave Europe the resources necessary to rebuild and gave the United States a way to avoid a new economic crisis on the scale of the Great Depression, must still be considered one of the most intelligent political and economic actions in human history. One may speak of these twenty-five years as a period of positive imperialism.

The United States, fixated as it was on the "cold war" against communism and a little overconfident about the permanence and naturalness of its economic preeminence, gave absolute priority during the postwar years to securing political allegiance within the sphere that it already dominated militarily. To further this goal, it opened its markets to European products as well as to those from Japan, thus sacrificing, without at first being aware of it and subsequently with real anxiety, large sectors of its industrial base. The trade deficit with Japan first appeared at the beginning of the 1970s. It has since spread to the entire globe—in other words, well beyond the original sphere of political domination.

The collapse of communism has permitted new and important countries to enter into this asymmetrical system of exchange. Today it is China, not Japan, which has the largest trade surplus with the United States. America's superconsumption has now become a crucial element in a global economic structure that is considered by some to be imperial. It is not America's productivity that is essential within a world economy where demand is sluggish but, rather, its consumption. This new situation is a structural outcome of certain free-trade policies.

THE KEYNESIAN STATE OF A DEPRESSED WORLD ECONOMY

In conformity with classical economic theory, the general opening up of commercial exchange has brought about an increase in inequality throughout the world. This general exchange tends to introduce into each country the same disparities in revenue that exist at the level of the whole planet. Throughout the world international competition has led to the stagnation of wages and substantial increases in profits. The compression of worker revenues caused by free trade revives the traditional dilemma of capitalism that has now spread across the globe: low salaries do not allow for the absorption of increases in production. This elementary phenomenon was studied in England by Malthus and later by Keynes as well as by most socialist economists of the nineteenth and twentieth centuries. It is also understood perfectly well by the nonconformist economists in the United States.

The economists of the American university establishment generally acknowledge the rise in inequality caused by free trade. The drop off in demand, however, is a taboo subject even for fake nonconformists such as Paul Krugman. To point out this effect of globalization is to break ranks with the established order, and only true rebels such as Chalmers Johnson will take such a risk. His book, *Blowback: The Costs and Consequences of American Empire*, is one of the cruelest studies of American behavior since the Second World War.[7] Robert Gilpin, on the other hand— although a lucid analyst of globalization, aware of the persistence of states and nations and of the structural differences between the capitalist systems in Japan, Germany, and the Anglo-Saxon countries, and attentive to the economic and ideological fragility of American hegemony—does not dare bring up this problem for it would mean breaking the good behavior code set down by the Establishment.

I am being slightly unfair to Joseph Stiglitz, the former leading economist of the World Bank, and unquestionably a member of the Establishment for which his Nobel Prize serves as a kind of official membership card. In *Globalization and Its Discontents* (2002), Stiglitz underlines the problem of general worldwide demand and mentions repeatedly the International Monetary Fund's (IMF) inability to see the insufficiencies of national demand or even regional demand, notably in Asia.[8] But Stiglitz remains loyal to free-trade principles and practically speaking can only wring his hands about the lack of instruments for global regulation. I cannot tell if he is naïve or coy, perhaps both: tough on the bureaucrats of the IMF but faithful to the dogma of his profession. We ought not be absurdly demanding—the fact that one of the leading American authorities on economics claims, fol-

lowing Keynes, that a slowdown in global demand is possible and
that it is necessary to contemplate regulatory mechanisms on a
global scale is itself a turning point, even if, given the current situation, the government in Washington is unlikely to be able to
act on such a proposal.

The tendency toward sluggish demand that results from free
trade and low salaries is plain to see, and it explains the regular
decrease in growth rates of the world economy and the increasingly frequent recessions. None of this is new; however, we ought
to extend our study so as to take account of the strategic implications of a drop in worldwide consumption for the United States
today. It is the stagnation of demand on a global scale that allows
the United States to justify its role as the regulator and predator
of the globalized economy, in effect to claim for itself the lead
role in a planetary Keynesian state.>

In a slowed down, depressed world economy, America's
propensity to consume more than it produces ends up being
viewed by the rest of the planet as something positive, even mer-
itorious. In every recession, we enthusiastically praise the persistent dynamism of American consumption, such that it becomes
the fundamental positive characteristic of an economy whose
fundamental nonproductivity we no longer wish to see. The percentage of income saved by American households is next to zero.
But every "economic recovery" of the United States increases the
importation of goods from around the world. The negative trade
balance deepens and deepens, breaking every year the record low
of the year before. But we are happy and relieved. Ours is the
world of La Fontaine's fable turned upside down: today the ant
pleads with the grasshopper to agree to take more of its food.

We behave toward the United States like Keynesian global citizens who are expecting the state to jump start the economy.
Indeed, according to Keynes, one of the purposes of the state is to
support demand through consumption. In his *General Theory*
Keynes has a kind word for the pharaohs who built the pyramids,

big spenders who thereby regulated economic activity.[9] Our pyramid is America—kept intact by the work of the entire planet. One can note the absolute compatibility of this vision of America as the key state within a Keynesian world and the political interpretation of globalization. According to this model the trade deficit of the United States ought to be called an imperial levy.

From an economic point of view American society has become *the* state of the entire planet. It often expresses its own hostility to the state, however, an attitude that it puts into practice through efforts to limit the state's role in the national economy, such as with Reagan-style deregulation. Paradoxically, the negation of the state in the society has ended up making a state of the society. Moreover, it is an entity that has, on the one hand, the negative characteristics that classical or neoclassical economists attribute to the state, namely nonproductivtity and financial irresponsibility; and on the other, the positive potential the Keynesian economists concede to the state, namely the capacity to stimulate demand in times of depression.

The monetary and psychological mechanisms are obscure, but today's Americans, so dynamic and so capable of accepting the insecurity of a deregulated work world, have become *en masse* the planet's nonproductive, ever-consuming government employees. An excess of individual responsibility has only generated a collective irresponsibility. >

THE "IMPERIAL" RESHAPING OF AMERICAN SOCIETY

This "imperial" evolution of the economy, one that has certain analogies with the Roman Empire after the conquest of the Mediterranean region, has affected different parts of American society in different ways. Industry and the working class, that until recently had been considered as part of the middle class, were hit extremely hard. Their partial disintegration is reminiscent of the peasantry and artisan classes of Rome that were mostly destroyed by the influx of agricultural products and other goods from Sicily, Egypt, and Greece. Along the same lines American workers from 1970 to 1990 experienced relative or absolute pauperization.

Without going into the details of the economic mechanisms or beyond a certain level of generality, one can simply note that the imperial changes of the economy tend to transform the upper strata of American society into the upper strata of an imperial society (or "global" to use the current expression) that goes beyond the contours of the nation. This imperializing, or "globalizing" society first integrated all of what was called the "Free World" and then, after the fall of communism, virtually the totality of the planet.

In the United States, the portion of "national" income that falls to the richest 5 percent has increased from 15.5 percent in 1980 to 21.9 percent in 2000, the portion of the richest 20 percent from 43.1 percent to 49.4 percent. The portion of the remaining 80 percent has fallen from 56.9 percent to 50.6 percent. Each of the following lower four-fifths has seen their income fall—from 24.7 percent to 22.9 percent, from 17.1 percent to 14.9 percent, from 10.6 percent to 9.0 percent, and 4.5 percent to 3.7 percent, respectively. According to the rankings published in *Forbes* magazine, the four hundred wealthiest Americans for the year 2000 were collectively ten times richer than the four hundred wealthiest Americans of 1990 even though the GNP had only doubled. The stupendous swelling of incomes in the upper layer of American society cannot be explained otherwise than with the imperial model, and the same goes for the sluggish or very slow income growth of the vast majority of the population.

Grouping these statistics in two columns so as to represent the 1980–1984 changes and the 1994–2000 changes side by side shows that the increase in income disparities is not constant, but instead corresponds to a sort of phase 1 of imperial reorganization.

TABLE 5. Evolution of Personal Income in the United States

Average Income in Adjusted Dollars	1980	1994	2000	1980/1994	1994/2000
The richest 5%	132,551	210,684	250,146	+59%	+19%
The richest 20% (1st fifth)	91,624	121,943	141,620	+33%	+16%
2nd fifth	52,169	58,005	65,729	+11%	+13%
3rd fifth	34,431	37,725	42,361	+5%	+14%
4th fifth	21,527	22,127	25,334	+3%	+14%
5th fifth	8,920	8,934	10,190	+0%	+14%

SOURCE: http://www.census.gov/hhes/income/hisinc/h03.html

Between 1980 and 1994 the greatest increases in income went to those who were already among the richest—59 percent for the wealthiest 5 percent—and the increases are smaller and smaller as one descends, with the poorest 20 percent experiencing zero growth over the same period. This is truly a dramatic increase in inequality.

However, between 1994 and 2000, the evolution changes significantly: the rise of inequality almost stops. The growth of revenues at the upper level weakened, with only a 19 percent increase for the top 5 percent, and all the other groups, including the bottom 20 percent, experienced almost identical increases of 13 percent to 16 percent. The apologists for the "New Economy" claim to see in the latter changes the egalitarian phase of a modernization process that would necessarily include in a first phase a period of increased inequality—so goes one of the favorite theories within the snug world of Harvard's economics department.

If we pursue the analogy with Roman history, we cannot help but notice a striking coincidence between this phase 2 of the recent evolution of American society—characterized by greater equality in income growth—and the enormous swelling of the U.S. trade deficit that went from slightly less than 100 billion dollars per year in 1993 to 450 billion dollars in 2000. Once the system of imperial levies on material goods has become fully operational the whole population can profit from it.

Between 1970 and 2000 the United States underwent a process of social polarization of the Roman type—it combines the development of a plutocracy and the expansion of the plebeian class in the sense that this term had during the Roman Empire. The terms *plutocracy* and *plebeian* are not just metaphors for characterizing the income levels of the elite and the mass; rather, they serve to recall that this wealth, great or small, does not derive from a directly productive activity but is instead the effect of political domination of the outside world.[10]

In the next chapter I will discuss the rather mysterious mechanisms by which this wealth is siphoned off and redistributed within a liberal economy, but I insist here on the pertinence of the Roman comparison. Between 1994 and 2000, America has reached the stage of "bread and circuses" not the miracle of the "new economy" promised by road signs along the "information superhighway."

(Of course I am exaggerating slightly so as to make my point perfectly clear. The economists who want to believe in the genuine efficiency and real productivity of the American economy are not completely unreasonable. At the present time the only unreasonable thing is the absence or, more accurately, the disappearance of the public debate that was going on from 1990 to 1995—a debate in which a certain skepticism about the true efficiency of the American economy was at least able to exist as an opposing view in competition with the general orthodoxy.)

If one turns from models to historical reality, one could say that America hesitated over the course of the last twenty years between two types of social and economic organization: the nation and the empire. The country has by no means lost all of its national characteristics, and it will fail as an empire. But it is clear that there was an acceleration in the imperial direction between 1990 and 2000, and especially from 1994 to 2000.

The American Trade Deficit (in Billions of Dollars)

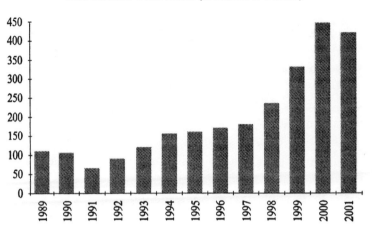

SOURCE: http://www.census.gov/foreign trade

NATION VS. EMPIRE: THE DEBATE OF 1990—1995

The choice of an imperial economic policy did not happen without debate or conflict. There were in fact more researchers in America than in Europe who denounced free trade and its consequences for the American working class, though often, it is true, these voices spoke from outside the generally orthodox environment that reigns within prestigious universities. The United States can be credited with the rediscovery of Friedrich List, a German theoretician of protectionism, who put forward the idea of a national economic space protected from the outside world but liberal when it comes to its internal functioning.[11] So-called strategic traders, who favored a defense of American industry against Asia in general and Japan in particular, published numerous texts and had a certain political importance during the first Clinton administration.

Strategic traders understood the problems from the perspective of economics and commerce. In 1995 Michael Lind was the first to elaborate a complete vision of the evolution of an American society given over to free trade. He did not simply denounce the squashing of the working class and other ordinary Americans. His most important contribution was to identify and describe the new American ruling class. He defined this "white overclass" not simply in terms of its wealth but by its cultural ways and habits of mind—its preference for legal studies over engineering, for example, a love for all things English, a certain perfidious indulgence toward "positive discrimination" to favor racial minorities while at the same time remaining adept at sliding their own children past the intellectual competition of the university environment. Lind has sketched the portrait of a stratified, less democratic America where, for example, unions no longer influence the Democratic party.[12] I believe he was the first to realize that at the present moment a reversal has taken place between Europe and the United States whereby the Old World has become more democratic than the New World.[13] Lind, an intellectual and activist, asked for a national redefinition of America that would be self-reliant and democratic rather than dependent and oligarchic.

That was in 1995. The increases in the American trade deficit between 1994 and 2000, along with the changes in income presented above, suggest that the fight for a democratic and economically independent nation was lost between 1995 and 2000. This chronology and the acceleration of the imperial dynamic that it implies cannot be understood separately from the clearly distinct but related evolution of America's historical rival and polar opposite, Russia. This will be discussed in my sixth chapter, devoted to the general logic of America's foreign policy. The movement of the United States toward a full-fledged imperial system does not depend solely or even most importantly on the power relations within American society. Empire implies above all else a relation to an outside world that must be dominated, absorbed, and transformed into an interior space that falls under the power of the state.

Will we, one day, speak of an American empire? Throughout history true empires have always presented two characteristics that are related to each other functionally. First, empire is born from military force, and that force permits the extraction of tribute that nourishes the imperial center. Second, the center ends up treating conquered peoples as ordinary citizens and inversely treating ordinary citizens like conquered peoples. The imperial power dynamic leads to the development of a universal egalitarianism whose origin is not the liberty of all but, rather, the common lot of their oppression. This universalism born of despotism engenders a feeling of common responsibility toward all subjects within a political space where there are essentially no longer any differences between the conquering people and the conquered.

These two criteria allow one to see immediately that Rome—first a conquering predator then a universal builder of roads, aqueducts, laws, and peace—well deserved the name "empire"; whereas the Greek version centered in Athens remained incomplete. One can give Athens the benefit of the doubt and say that the military force of its army's conquest is proved by the *phoros* or tribute paid by the cities in the Delian League. But Athens hardly advanced in a universalizing direction. At most, it took on the role of judging according to its own system of law certain legal conflicts that arose between allied cities of the league. However, it never extended its citizenship as Rome did. On the contrary, it tended to restrict it during the central power's period of affirmation.

If one applies each of these two criteria, there will certainly not be in, say 2050, an "American Empire" because the United States simply does not have what it takes to be a true empire. Two types of "imperial" resources are especially lacking in the American case. First, its power to constrain militarily and economically is insufficient for maintaining the current levels of exploitation of the planet; and second, its ideological universalism is in decline and does not allow it, as before, to treat individuals and whole peoples equally as the leading guarantor of their peace and prosperity. The next two chapters will examine these fundamental deficiencies.

4

The Fragility of Tribute

It is commonplace today to denounce the American military as disproportionately large, and its XXL size as a clear sign of the country's imperial ambitions. It has been pointed out, for example, that the military budget of the only remaining superpower represents one third of all military spending in the world. Do not expect America's leaders to openly doubt the strength of their army; however, a methodical examination of these expenses reveals that a genuine concern about the military capability of the United States led President Bush to propose budget increases even before September 11. We are dealing with an intermediate situation: the American military is way too big if one considers exclusively its own national security, but way too small to control an empire, and especially one that would seek to maintain lasting hegemonic control over Eurasia considering how far it is from the New World.

The fragility of the American military is in a sense structural—
a consequence of having never fought an adversary of its own size
at any time in its history. One may recall, for example, the form-
ative experience of the numerous wars against Native Americans.
These were radically asymmetrical confrontations between
underequipped and largely illiterate populations on one side, and
a modern, European-type army on the other.

A TRADITIONAL MILITARY WEAKNESS

From its origins, therefore, a curious sort of self-doubt hangs over
the reality of America's military vocation. The spectacular
deployment of economic resources during the Second World
War cannot make one forget the moderate success of the campaigns on the ground—aside from the Anglo-American air raids
that caused so many civilian casualties. These bombings had no
appreciable strategic affect, and no doubt their only important
consequence was the overall hardening of the resistance of the
German people against the Allied offensive.

The strategic truth of the Second World War is that it was won
on the Eastern European front by Russia. The latter's extensive
human sacrifices before and after Stalingrad eventually broke the
Nazi military machine. The Normandy invasion of June 1944
occurred late, after the Russian troops had already reached their
own western border in the direction of Germany. One cannot
understand the ideological confusion of the postwar period if one
forgets that in the minds of many at the time it was Russian communism that had defeated German Nazism and contributed
most to the liberation of Europe.

At every stage, as the historian and military expert Liddell Hart
has observed, the behavior of the American troops was bureau-
cratic, slow, and inefficient given the huge amounts of human
and economic forces they had committed.[1] Whenever it was pos-

sible, operations that demanded a certain spirit of sacrifice were handed over to Allied contingents—Polish and French at Monte Cassino in Italy, Polish for securing the poche de Falaise in Normandy. The current American "approach" in Afghanistan, which consists of hiring and paying tribal leaders on a freelance basis one operation at a time, is only the latest and most extreme version of an old method. In this regard, America resembles neither ancient Rome nor Athens but, rather, Carthage, which used to borrow the services of Gaulois mercenaries and the rabble from among the Balearic Islands. America's B-52s are today's elephants, but there is no Hannibal.

The mastery of the American navy and air force, on the other hand, is indisputable. This was already apparent in the Pacific campaign of the Second World War even if accounts of the confrontations between Japanese and Americans tend not to mention the significantly larger deployment of material force on the American side. After some early heroic battles such as Midway that pitted opposing forces of comparable size, the war in the Pacific began to resemble rather quickly an "Indian War" where the inequality of the technological forces led to extraordinarily unequal numbers of casualties.[2]

After the Second World War, every step that led the American army closer to a confrontation with Russia, the true winner on the ground in that war, revealed the fundamental fragility of the American military. In Korea, the United States was only half convincing, in Vietnam not at all. Fortunately, the real test against the Red army did not take place. As for the Gulf War, it was a victory over a myth: the Iraqi army, a military instrument of an underdeveloped country of twenty million inhabitants.

The recent circulation of the idea of a bloodless war, at least in the United States, is the culmination of an original preference for asymmetrical confrontations. This concept admits and gives formal validation to the traditional weakness of the American ground forces.

I am not accusing the United States of being unable to wage war like other countries—in other words, carrying out the mindless butchery of their adversaries and their own population. To wage war at the least cost to oneself and at the greatest cost for the enemy is arguably the result of a perfectly normal utilitarian logic. Nevertheless, the absence of a tradition of American military might on the ground makes it difficult if not impossible to occupy territory and establish a truly imperial space in the traditional sense.

Today, the Russian army has been reduced to a small fraction of its former superpower status. Anyone who wants to can raise mocking eyebrows at its difficulties in Chechnya. However, in the Caucasus region, Russia is showing that it can still exact levies of blood from its own population, and with the support of electors. In this way, the military is exercising one of its particular resources that is both social and psychological—something the United States is in the process of losing forever as it invests further in the notion of a bloodless war.

THE GEOGRAPHY OF THE "EMPIRE"

In 1998, ten years after the fall of the Soviet system and just before the start of the "war on terrorism," the distribution of American military forces around the world was still largely defined by that major conflict of the past, the Cold War. At that time, outside of the United States, there were 60,053 soldiers stationed in Germany, 41,257 in Japan, 35,663 in South Korea, 11,677 in Italy, 11,379 in Great Britain, 3,576 in Spain, 2,864 in Turkey, 1,679 in Belgium, 1,066 in Portugal, 703 in the Netherlands, and 498 in Greece.[3] This distribution of American forces and military installations offers a nonsubjective impression of something that resembles "empire." The two fundamental possessions of the

United States, their true hold over the Old World as Brzezinski has clearly pointed out, are the European and Far Eastern protectorates of Germany and Japan, two entities without which there could be no global American power. These two protectorates provide the lodging and most of the food for 85 percent of all American military personnel abroad.

Compared with these military strongholds, the new pole in southeastern Europe, including Hungary, Croatia, Bosnia, and Macedonia had 13,774 Americans deployed in 1998, and the deployment in the Middle East (in Egypt, Saudi Arabia, Kuwait, and Bahrain) was 9,956. Of course there is Turkey with 12,820 American troops, a multitask pole turned simultaneously toward Russia and toward the Middle East. But for the most part the empire's soldiers are standing guard on the margins of the former communist territory in a ring around Russia and China. The deployment of 12,000 troops in Afghanistan and 1,500 in Uzbekistan has completed rather than altered this fundamental geographic setup.

AN ABORTED WITHDRAWAL

The above description is not intended as a denunciation of a stable and persistent pattern of willful American aggression. It is even possible to make the opposite claim. During the ten years that followed the breakup of the Soviet empire, the United States faithfully played the card of decommissioning and downsizing. In 1990 the American military budget was 385 billion dollars, in 1998 only 280 billion—a 28 percent reduction. Between 1990 and 2000 the total number of active military personnel fell from 2 million to 1.4 million—a 32 percent reduction. No matter what the true nature of the GDP is, the percentage of it devoted to military spending went from 5.2 percent in 1990 to 3 percent in 1999. It is hard to see how such military cutbacks could be interpreted as

TABLE 6. American Military Personnel Abroad in 1998

Countries with More Than
200 U.S. Military Personnel

Germany	60,053
Japan	41,257
South Korea	35,663
Italy	11,677
Great Britain	11,379
Great Britain	11,379
Bosnia and Herzegovina	8,170
Egypt	5,846
Panama	5,400
Hungary	4,200
Spain	3,575
Turkey	2,864
Iceland	1,960
Saudi Arabia	1,722
Belgium	1,679
Kuwait	1,640
Cuba (Guantanamo)	1,527
Portugal	1,066
Croatia	866
Bahrain	748
Diego Garcia	705
The Netherlands	703
Macedonia	518
Greece	498
Honduras	427
Australia	333
Haiti	239
Total	259,871
Land	218,957
Sea	40,914

SOURCE: *Statistical Abstract of the United States: 2000*, p.368.

the unmistakable sign of an imperial will. To endlessly denounce a permanent American project for global domination is absurd. The cutbacks in American military spending did not stop before 1996–1998. After 1998 the military budget started going back up.

There are thus two identifiable phases whose existence signals a turnaround in U.S. strategy toward the end of the 1990s. Once again, we see that the period from 1990 to 2000 is not uniformly consistent.

Phase 1: Between 1990 and 1995 there was clearly an imperial withdrawal on the part of the military that coincided with the increasingly vigorous debate over protectionism and the possibility of choosing a national-democratic tack when it came to the country's socioeconomic orientation. In the wake of communism, a redefinition of the United States as a great nation and the leader of the liberal democracies but in principle equal to them was seriously contemplated. This choice would have included a return to relative economic independence. This would not mean self-sufficiency, or even the reduction of levels of foreign trade, but balanced exchanges of goods and services with neither large deficits nor large surpluses — in other words, embracing instead of trying to discredit a leading economic indicator of the equality of nations.

Phase 2: Little by little this option was pushed aside, or one could say it gradually failed. Between 1997 and 1999 the trade deficit increased exponentially. Between 1999 and 2001 America stopped making cutbacks and began remilitarizing. There is a necessary relation between the country's increased economic dependence and the renewed growth of its military. The redevelopment of the armed forces was the result of a growing awareness of America's increasing economic vulnerability.

The decision announced by George W. Bush to seek a 15 percent increase in military spending was made before the events of September 11. Roughly speaking, by 1999 the American political establishment realized the true inadequacy of its military potential should the economy become wholly of the imperial type with a consuming center dependent on a productive periphery. The security questions for a plundering country that lives off of the simple capture of outside riches are different from those that face a country that practices balanced trade in a spirit of give and take.

In the case of the United States, however, it is inaccurate to characterize its capture of wealth as tribute in the traditional, imperial, state-controlled sense of the term since tribute is obtained through direct violence and military constraint. Only the costs of room and board of the American military that are absorbed by Japan and Germany could be said to conform to this classical type of tribute. The way in which the United States manages to go on taking without giving is bizarre, mysterious, and dangerous.

THE STRANGENESS AND SPONTANEITY OF TRIBUTE

America imports and consumes. To pay for its imports, it draws to itself monetary resources from throughout the world, but in a way that is original and without precedent in the history of empires. Athens collected the *phoros*, an annual contribution of the allied cities, first given voluntarily and then demanded by force. Rome at first pillaged the treasuries of the Mediterranean world, then extorted, either through direct seizure or indirectly through the money collected through taxes, the wheat crops of Sicily and Egypt. Violent acts of levying were so inherent to Roman existence that Caesar admitted that he could not conquer Germanic lands because their instable itinerant agricultural practices were insufficient to nourish the Roman legions.

The United States does not use authoritarian methods to collect more than a small fraction of the monetary resources and other goods that it needs. There is, as we have noted, the "room and board" offered to American troops in Japan and Germany. During the Gulf War, there were direct financial contributions of the allied states, which, unlike France and Great Britain, did not participate in military operations. This was an example of something very close to the Athenian *phoros*. Finally, there is the export of arms. These are real goods, the sale of which does bring in money, but their value is not defined by the "preferences of individual consumers" to use the language of liberal economic theory. The power relations between states determine these sales and sometimes reveal the bargaining advantage of American muscle, a lesson that was recently learned by the naïve representatives of the French company Dassault in South Korea.[4]

The revenue that these arms sales brings into the United States is the equivalent of tribute collected by political and military means. But the volume of these sales is hardly enough to counterbalance the current levels of American consumption. Traditional anti-Americanism rightly underlines the overwhelming role of the United States as an arms exporter: 32 billion dollars in 1997, which represents 58 percent of all international arm sales. In military terms this percentage is phenomenal. When the trade deficit was only 180 billion dollars, the 32 billion in sales was economically significant; however, it does not amount to much now that the trade deficit has ballooned to 450 billion dollars in 2000.

The control of certain petroleum producing zones is an important component of traditional tribute. The dominant position, both politically and economically, of multinational American oil companies allows the United States to extort a global annuity, but here again one that is insufficient to offset the American importation of goods of all kinds. However, the dominant role of oil within the system of political levies sheds light on the obsessive fixation of American foreign policy on this particular commodity.

Finally, the majority of tribute that is obtained by the United States flows to it freely and spontaneously without political or military force. American purchases of goods from throughout the world are paid for. In a money market that is freer than it ever was, American economic agents collect foreign currency to pay for these purchases. To do this, they buy this foreign capital with dollars, the magical currency that never lost its value during the years of worsening budget deficits, at least until April of 2002. This persistent strength of the dollar was so magical that certain economists concluded that the economic role of the United States in the world was no longer to produce goods like other countries but instead to provide money.

THE O'NEILL DOCTRINE

In the world imagined by economic theory, the demand for foreign currency necessary to buy foreign goods ought to bring about a decline in the value of the dollar, a currency no longer so important for the purchase of American goods now less and less competitive in the global market. Such movements were observed in the 1970s when the trade deficit first appeared. Contrary to what certain French traditionalists may think, the dollar's role as reserve currency does not shield America's buying power from the negative consequences of its weak performance as an exporter.

And yet, twenty-five years later, at the beginning of this new millennium, the American dollar has remained fairly strong despite having the largest deficit in world history, relatively low interest rates, and an inflation rate higher than that of both Europe and Japan. Why? Because the world's money has tended to flow to the United States. Everywhere, companies, banks, and institutional as well as private investors decided to buy dollars thus keeping its value high. In this context these dollars do not serve to purchase consumer goods; instead, they allow direct investment in the United States or indirect investment through treasury bonds, as well as corporate stocks and bonds.

It is the movement of financial capital that guarantees the American balance of payments. In simple terms, year after year the movement of capital from outside to the inside of the United States allows American "insiders" to buy goods from the rest of the outside world. If one recalls that the majority of imported goods purchased are intended for consumption that is infinitely renewable in the short term while on the other hand the capital invested in the United States is placed there with a view toward short- or long-term goals, it must be said that there is something paradoxical if not to say structurally unstable about this circular mechanism.

After repeated declarations by the American treasury secretary, *The Economist* of London elegantly but somewhat nervously decided to call the thesis that in a world without borders a proper trade balance was no longer of any importance "The O'Neill Doctrine."[5] Felix Rohatyn, a former U.S. ambassador to France, expressed more baldly the worry of American leaders when, in response to the Enron scandal and its possible negative effects on foreign investment, he underlined that America needs 1 billion dollars of inflowing capital every day to pay for its trade deficit.[6]

The American Bureau of Economic Analysis follows with some anxiety the annual "cover-up" of import expenses by means of influxes of capital. So long as national currencies exist, the balance has to be established one way or another. The reassuring speeches of O'Neill—who was singing nonsense lullabies to the financial markets—could only make sense in a truly imperial monetary universe; that is if the dollar had an enforced exchange rate for the entire planet, a situation that could only come about through absolute military force and state control. In other words, it would take a Weberian monopoly on legitimate domination exercised by the United States on a global scale.[7] The American army that has captured neither Mullah Omar nor Osama Bin Laden would seem rather incapable of fulfilling such a role. The traditional rules remain valid: if the Americans consume too much and the influx of capital ceases, the dollar will crash. But perhaps my thinking is incorrectly based on a totally archaic conception of empire and power and I have accorded too much importance to the notion of political and military constraint. At this stage of globalized capitalism, the influx of capital may have become an intrinsic necessity—the stable element within a new type of imperial economy. This is a possibility that needs to be considered.

A SUPERPOWER LIVING HAND TO MOUTH

The dominant interpretation offered by economists who do not want to make waves (either because they belong to the American university establishment or because they work for companies that live off the transfer of funds) claims that foreign investment in the United States happens because the American economy is more dynamic, understands and accepts risk, and in a strict sense proves more profitable. OK, why not? The "physical" nonproductivity of the technological and industrial bases within an economy such as that of the United States does not alone mean that the financial rewards to be reaped will be small. In principle it is not difficult to conceive of an economy that would be able to function for a rather long but finite period with, on the one hand, substantial increases in corporate profits and, on the other, the overdevelopment of useless areas of production. It is possible for financial service companies to run on their own steam generating profits from operations that have nothing to do with real production. We have already seen that the financial services sector has become more important than industry in the American economy. In short, a high level of profits in areas that are not "physically" productive can lead the economy toward nonproductivity. The brokerage activities of Enron were, from this point of view, the archetype, since the point was to make money from an intermediate operation that was not directly productive but one that would, in theory, "optimize" the relations between production and consumption. As one used to be able to say before the advent of the Internet and E-commerce, the proof is in the pudding. In the case of Enron, it is now clear that there was never was any pudding, only a pudding substitute cooked up by Arthur Andersen. But the euphoria surrounding Enron really existed, and it shaped, for a few years, the direction of the real economy, leading it toward underproduction and an energy deficit.

To say that money flows to the United States because investors naturally want to maximize the return on their investment is to buy into the ruling dogma of our time that says rich people are always drawn to high risk/high reward opportunities. However, if this were what was motivating rich people—the love of profits and a taste for risk—a dominant share of stock purchases and direct investment would be made outside the United States. But this is not the case. All the capital flowing to the United States is not going there because of enthusiastic visions about a "New Economy" and "Information Superhighways." As we shall see, the search for a safe haven is considered more important than profitability.

The most surprising thing for anyone who is interested in the equilibrium of America's balance of payments is the variability of the positions held by purchases of treasury bonds, corporate stocks, corporate bonds, or by direct investments that go to financing the American deficit.[8] These wildly changing movements cannot be explained by changes in interest rates since the latter do not happen at the same pace or to the same degree. The purchases of treasury bonds and other private company bonds no doubt obey the profitability imperative but they show a preference for the security of fixed returns on investment that are guaranteed by a reliable political, economic, banking, and monetary system. These conservative purchases have been and still are very important for the day-to-day financing of the United States.

We may leave out the important but instable and mysterious role of various debts, banking and nonbanking, and concentrate our analysis on the classical and comforting aspects surrounding the movement of investment capital. Let us also concentrate on the decisive decade of the 1990s during which the world wrote the epitaph of the communist era and completed the apotheosis of financial globalization. The huge and rapid increase of capital flows to the United States was staggering—from 88 billion dollars in 1990, it ballooned to 865 billion in 2001. These figures of course do not take into account the reverse movement, about half the size, of capital moving out of the United States. A positive balance of 485 billion dollars was necessary in 2000 to offset the trade deficit in goods and services. But beyond the growing mass of immigrant investment capital, the most striking thing about this decade is the changing mix in types of investment. In 1990 direct investment dominated with the creation or purchase of companies in America by foreigners (55 percent of total foreign investment). In 1991 the purchase of stocks and bonds took the lead, representing 45 percent of all foreign investment. In the years 1991–1992 and 1995–1997 the purchase of U.S. Treasury bonds was strong and served to cover the American budget deficit. Between 1997 and 2001 the purchase of stocks and bonds of individual companies took off, increasing from 28 percent to 58 percent of all foreign investment. One could believe that the world is experiencing the consecration of liberal capital, circulating accurately and efficiently thanks to billions of small transactions in international money markets. However, if, as is possible for the years 2000 and 2001, we look separately at figures for the purchase of stocks of variable profitability and those for bonds with fixed rates of return, we discover that the dominant heroic scenario of seeking maximum profit through maximum risk taking, normally associated with the purchase of stocks, does not correspond to what has really happened.

At their height in 2000 the purchase of American stocks by foreigners totaled 192.7 billion dollars, but in the same year the total value of bonds purchased totaled 292.9 billion. If we measure these figures as a percentage of the total amount of new money siphoned off by the United States from the rest of the world, we get 19 percent for stocks and 30 percent for bonds. In 2001, a year of recession and the terrorist attacks, the volume represented by

TABLE 7. Foreign Purchases of Stock and Direct Investment
in the United States

	Total in Millions of Dollars	Treasury Bonds %	Stocks and Bonds %	Direct Investment %	Debts%
1990	88,861	-3	2	55	46
1991	78,020	24	45	30	1
1992	116,786	32	26	17	26
1993	191,387	13	42	27	19
1994	243,006	14	23	19	43
1995	343,504	29	28	17	26
1996	441,952	35	29	20	16
1997	715,472	20	28	15	37
1998	507,790	10	43	35	12
1999	747,786	-3	46	40	16
2000	985,470	-5	49	29	27
2001	865,584	2	58	18	22

SOURCE: http://www.bea.doc.gov/bea/international

the purchase of stock fell to 15 percent; however, the bond market took on new prominence, jumping from 30 percent to 43 percent of the total influx of capital to the United States.

The result of this analysis is, no pun intended, capital. Keynes got it right when he said that the man who wants to invest his money is plagued by a double anxiety—the fear of losing everything and the fear of not getting the highest possible return on his investment. Contrary to the dogmas of modern neoliberal ideology, the true history of recent investment reveals a predominant tendency toward safety and security when it comes to investing in the United States. This fact takes us away from the myths of liberal capitalism but closer to an imperial political logic under a globalized system of economics and finance, since the United States is definitely the political heart of the economic system and seemed until recently to be the most secure place to put one's money. The recent insecurity has everything to do with the accounting frauds in the United States and is hardly a product of September 11.

One problem, however, remains unresolved. The whole world has preferred to invest its money in the United States. Fine. But how is it that the planet has all this money to invest? The mechanism is fairly simple: globalization implies a massive increase in profits within each national society.

A STATE FOR THE RICH

Even if one admits (as I do) that capitalism is the only reasonable economic system, one has to concede that, left to itself, it tends to go off the rails in some fundamental ways that hurt everyone, including the rich. Let us try here to offer a truly impartial picture of what happens. Let us forget about the working poor and their low salaries for the moment; let us also forget the idea of the common good that has been ignored amidst the decline in global demand. Let us put on for once the spectacles of the truly privileged and force ourselves to be myopic and look closely at their principal concern—the future of their profits.

Increases in profitability raise incomes for the upper classes, but these swollen revenues are in no way a material reality. The mass of profits is an abstract sum, not "liquid" but "on paper" as one used to say before computer trading—tied up in a variety of investment instruments that the owners can in no way apply to their direct consumption. They can increase their spending on personnel and thus redistribute toward the lower strata of the society a part of their winnings. This practice is already very widespread in the United States, where the evolution is not toward a more modern service sector but instead a return to the human comedy of an "upstairs downstairs" master/servants economy that was common in earlier aristocratic societies. The titled aristocrats who possessed the wealth back then supported a passel of servants who did domestic tasks or fought against the nobleman's enemies. The new plutocracy has updated the butler with the lawyer, the accountant, and the personal bodyguard. The best analyses of these mechanisms of redistribution were done by the early English economists such as Smith who were all still able to witness at the end of the eighteenth century a downward redistribution of wealth through the massive employment of servants. "A man grows rich by employing a multitude of manufacturers; he grows poor by maintaining a multitude of menial servants."[9]

But the fortunes being amassed today are too enormous. We have already noted the spectacular increases of the percentage of total U.S. income garnered by the wealthiest 20 percent and even more so by the wealthiest 5 percent. To a lesser degree this phenomenon is also occurring in all countries that are a part of the globalized economy. What does one do with "unemployed" money? How does one keep it from disappearing? Or, expressed less anxiously and more hopefully, how does one make it work so that it will be fruitful and multiply all on its own?

Investment is a necessity. To be more precise, the existence of a secure context for the crystallization of profits, like sugar water to make rock candy, is an ontological necessity for capitalism. The state's role as borrower was perfectly understood by Marx. Public government expenditures were an early financial security tool of the bourgeoisie. Then there was the stock exchange where the profits amassed could be deposited. In a few short years global capitalism has landed us back in a wilderness situation. Over this time the top country for investment and the central state in the new economic system has enjoyed an initial comparative advantage for absorbing, for the sake of conservation and security, the expanded volume of world profits. America has had everything going for it—the right ideology, the largest military, and the largest initial public offerings. Japan aside, stock market capitalization among the other Western countries around 1990 was miniscule compared to what was happening in the United States. With an economic system that remains national and protectionist and a language that serves as a sort of natural barrier, Japan could not be a serious rival.

As *the* monetary and military leader, the United States offered, at first, unparalleled conditions for maximum security. Wall Street, where the leading indexes seem now to directly influence the trend of markets worldwide (up yesterday, down today), has become the endpoint of this security seeking mechanism—3,059 billion dollars invested in U.S. markets in 1990, 13,451 billion in 1998. But none of this has much to with the notion of economic performance considered in terms of real, physical productivity—even if the mantra of "new technologies" is a part of the process.

This increase in stock market capitalization that is totally disproportionate to the real growth of the American economy is nothing more than a sort of inflation of the rich. The extraction of profits swells incomes that are then poured into the market where the relative scarcity of the "goods" to be bought—stocks—produces increases in their nominal value.

VOLATILITY . . . OR, NOW YOU SEE IT, NOW YOU DON'T

The exploitation of the laboring classes in the developed world and the overexploitation of developing countries would not pose an insurmountable problem for the equilibrium of the globalized society if the ruling class of all the countries of the world, specifically the European and Japanese protectorates, could feel satis-

TABLE 8. Stock Market Capitalization (in Billions of Dollars)

	1990	1998	*Percentage Increase*
United States	3,059	2,496	340%
Japan	2,918	2,496	-15%
Great Britain	849	2,374	180%
Germany	355	1,094	208%
France	314	992	216%
Canada	2421	543	124%
Italy	149	570	283%

SOURCE: *Statistical Abstract of the United States: 2000*, table 1401.

fied. The growing vulnerability of American hegemony derives in part from the fact that the regulating mechanism is becoming a threat to the privileged classes within the dominated periphery, especially Europeans and Japanese but also the new bourgeoisie in developing countries. Now we should concentrate on following the global fate of profit, a path that will lead us beyond the mere moral denunciation of how it is skimmed off toward an understanding of its evaporation.

If we would get away from thinking in terms of a general abstract model and the antigravity vocabularies of capitalism, profits, the wealthy, the stock market, etc. and instead ground these notions in the reality of the world, we could say quite simply that a large portion of global profits flows toward the American stock and bond markets. I have no desire to retrace all the large and small paths by which foreign capital arrives and is redistributed in the United States. Their sheer complexity and the sometimes willfully misleading characterization of this or that financial procedure make the system into an endless labyrinth where one comes across hordes of lawyers and accountants working in this corner on behalf of the owners of capital, over there on the problems of indebtedness of the middle class, and in a third area the succession of purges on Wall Street. And one must not forget the constant lowering of interest rates—now to practically zero—which means in a speculative economy the free distribution of currency. But if we agree that the American economy is weak when it comes to real, physical productivity, as the massive and still growing levels of imports of consumer goods would suggest, then one has to conclude that the capitalization of the American stock and bond markets is a fiction and therefore the money that is traveling to the United States is literally traveling to a mirage and not the true oasis that many take it for.

By a myriad of mysterious ways, the money that the privileged on the periphery send to the United States as a capital investment is transformed by the Americans into monetary means that fuel the ongoing consumption of goods purchased throughout the world. Therefore, in one way or another, the capital investment ought to evaporate. Economics, if it is a science, ought to be able to theorize, analyze, and predict. The fall of the major stock market indexes, the disappearance of Enron, and the implosion of the audit and accounting firm of Arthur Andersen offer some clues worth thinking about. And of course in France, whether one thinks of the Crédit Lyonnais scandal or the pro-American megalomania of Jean-Marie Messier, the news of massive investment in the United States usually spells disaster. We do not yet know how and how fast European and Japanese investors will lose their shirts, but they will. The most likely scenario is a stock market crash larger than any we have experienced thus far that will be followed by the meltdown of the dollar—a one-two punch that would put an end to any further delusions of "empire" when it comes to the U.S. economy. We cannot yet say whether the decline of the dollar that began in April of 2002 in the wake of the Enron-Andersen affair is just a small hiccup in the system or the beginning of the end. Nothing of the kind was either wished or planned, and surely the breakdown of the machine will be just as surprising as was its emergence.

Insofar as the incomes of the poor, the middle class, and the wealthy advanced at roughly the same rate between 1995 and 2000, a moralist might take some comfort in observing the end result whereby an American plebeian takes hold of a portion of the world's profits, especially European profits. One might think of it as the elevation of the actions of Robin Hood into a religion—one steals from the rich to give to the poor, one's own poor! Are such practices not the very proof of an American imperial power comparable to Rome's?

One must recall that America does not possess the military strength of Rome. Its power over the world cannot be exercised without the agreement of the tributary ruling classes on the periphery. Beyond a certain rate of levies and a certain level of financial insecurity, belonging to an American empire is perhaps no longer the most reasonable course for these periphery states.

Their voluntary servitude will only be sustained so long as the United States treats its citizens fairly, or to be more precise, treats them more and more as members of the dominant central society as is consistent with one of the two basic principles of empire. The United States must win the periphery's allegiance through its universalism—by its words as much as by its economic deeds—to the idea that "we are all Americans."[10] But rather than feeling more and more American, we non-Americans are increasingly being treated as second-class citizens because, unfortunately for the rest of the world, a decline in universalism has become the central ideological tendency of America today.

5

The Movement Away from Universalism

One of the essential forces of empires, a principle behind both their dynamism and stability, is universalism, the capacity to treat all men and peoples as equals. A universalist attitude allows for the continuous extension of the system of power through the integration into the central fold of all conquered individuals and peoples. The initial ethnic base is erased. The size of the human mass that identifies with the imperial system endlessly increases because that system allows the conquered to redefine themselves as conquerors. In the minds of those who have submitted, the initial violence of the conqueror comes to be viewed as generosity.

The success of Rome and the failure of Athens, as we have seen, did not result from differing military aptitudes so much as it did from the gradual opening up of Roman citizenship and the gradual narrowing of Athenian citizenship. The Athenian people remained an ethnic group defined by blood—after 451 B.C. both parents had to be citizens in order for the children to belong. The Roman people, on the other hand, proud as any ethnic group, nevertheless expanded continuously to include first the population of Latium, then all of Italy, and finally the entire Mediterranean region. In 212 B.C. the edict of Emperor Caracalla gave Roman citizenship to all free inhabitants of the empire. In time the majority of Roman emperors came from the provinces.

There have been other examples of universalist systems where egalitarian treatment of men and peoples greatly expanded their military potential. They include China, which has the largest number of men ever united under one state power; the first Arab empire, whose rapid growth was due to the extreme egalitarianism within Islam, the military force of its conquerors, and the weakening of the Roman and Parthian states; and France and the Soviet Union in the modern era. The Soviet empire, though swept away by its economic fragility, relied on its capacity to treat all peoples equally—something that seems originally to have been native to the Russian people rather than a consequence of the ideological superstructure of communism. Before its demographic decline France was almost a true empire, one that, thanks to a universalist code, nearly ruled across the European continent. Among recent imperial failures, one can note the case of Nazism, a system whose radical ethnocentrism prevented the initial German force from multiplying its strength with the supplementary power of conquered groups.

A comparative examination suggests that the ability of a conquering people to treat conquered groups in an egalitarian manner does not result from external factors but derives instead from a specific anthropological code—a cultural predisposition that is present or absent. Peoples with an egalitarian conception of family relations, one where brothers especially are treated as equals, as is the case for Rome, China, the Arab world, Russia, and northern France, tend to perceive men and peoples as equal. An inclination toward integration results from this egalitarian cultural predisposition. Peoples whose traditional family structures do not include a strict definition concerning the equality of brothers, as was the case in Athens and even more clearly in Germany, do not succeed in developing an egalitarian attitude toward other men and peoples. In these cases military contact tends more often to reinforce an ethnically based self-identity as conqueror. What emerges is a fragmented rather than a homogeneous vision of humanity, a differentialist attitude rather than one of universalism.

Anglo-Saxons are hard to place along the axis of difference-based versus universalist thinking. The English are clearly differentialist if one considers how they have managed to preserve Welsh and Scottish identities for centuries. The British Empire, which established itself overseas thanks to overwhelming technological superiority, lasted only a short while. It made no effort to assimilate conquered peoples. The English made a specialty of indirect rule that did not endanger local customs. Their period of decolonization was relatively painless and a model of pragmatism because there was never any question of seeking to transform Indians, Africans, or Malaysians into cookie-cutter equivalents of the typical British citizen. The French, many of whom dreamed of turning Vietnamese and Algerians into ordinary Frenchmen, had more difficulty accepting the turning of their imperial tide. Their latent universalist predisposition induced them to practice a kind of imperial resistance that led to a succession of military and political disasters.

One must not, however, exaggerate the preference for difference among the English. When one recalls the modest size of Shakespeare's "blessed plot, this earth, this realm, this England," one has to say the vast dimensions of the British Empire, even if it was not long lasting, testify to a certain aptitude for treating conquered peoples in a way that was relatively egalitarian and decent. The classic studies in British social anthropology by Evans-Pritchard (on the Nuer of Sudan) and Meyer Fortes (on the Tallensi of Ghana), both models of rigor and sensitivity, were produced during the colonial period.[1] Their analyses combine the traditional English talent for describing ethnic differences with a keen perception of the universal human feelings hidden by the diversity of cultural structures. Anglo-Saxon individualism always allows for the possibility of direct contact with the individual conceived as man in general rather than man fashioned by the anthropological system.

In the case of America, one has the extreme form of the Anglo-Saxon ambivalence when it comes to the competing conceptions of differentialism versus universalism. The United States could be described in one sense as the outcome of a radical universalism on a national scale. After all, American society resulted from a fusion of immigrant populations from all over Europe. The original English core showed a brilliant capacity for absorbing individuals with differing ethnic backgrounds. Immigration from Central and Southern Europe declined after the 1920s, but the flow of immigrants to America resumed in the 1960s with this time large populations coming from Asia and Central and South America. The capacity to integrate and expand the center has been a key to America's success and is the most convincing element when it comes to measuring the country's imperial stature. The growth of the population, from 285 million in 2001 to an expected 346 million in 2025, is itself clear evidence of America's talent for expansion.

However, the United States can also be described in the opposite way as a radically differentialist country. In American history there is always an unassimilable group, different and "other," that is condemned either to destruction or, as is more often the case, to segregation. Indians and blacks have played this role right down to being recast as composite or hyphenated Americans now known as "Native Americans" and "African Americans." African Americans continue to play the role of the different group today, as does the Indian or Native American population that has now expanded to include "Hispanic" and "Latino/Latina" populations as well. The American ideological system synthesizes uni-

versalism and differentialism into a totality: apparently contradictory theoretical assumptions turn out in practice to function in
complementary ways. In the beginning there is uncertainty about
the "other" whom one does not know whether to define as similar or different from oneself. Some strangers will be perceived as
similar and hence equal, others as truly other, which means here
different and inferior. Similarity and difference, equality and
inferiority arise together through polarization. The rejection of
Indians and blacks (if we may keep to the names commonly used
before the hyphenation movement of the last twenty years)
allowed Irish, German, Jewish, and Italian immigrants to be
treated as equals. By the same token, the definition of these latter
groups of immigrants as equals allowed for considering Indians
and blacks as inferior.

The Anglo-Saxon uncertainty when it comes to determining
the status of the "other" is not a consequence of modernity. On
the contrary, it would seem to be the legacy of a primitive anthropological condition having to do with England's peripheral position, historically and culturally speaking, on the border of the
Old World. This peripheral position may have led to its being
weakly or badly integrated into the empires that succeeded one
another to the south and east, and thus not being able or willing
to master the principles of equality and inequality. This primitive
condition only pertains to family relations and anthropological
values—it has not at all prevented England and America from
being pioneers of economic modernity in the most recent phase
of world history.

English culture is therefore characterized by a certain blurry
lack of definition around the values of equality and inequality, a
condition that contrasts sharply with the general clarity on these
matters in Eurasia.[2] If we return to the model that associates
anthropological structures and ideological preconceptions, we
can identify in the traditional English family a lack of definition
on the ideological level—English brothers are different, neither

equal nor unequal. Compared to the inegalitarian inheritance rules that apply among the German and Japanese and the egalitarian rules among the French, Russians, Arabs, and Chinese, one notes the English parents' wide margin of freedom to decide for themselves how to divide their wealth among their children by means of a written will. Outside of the English aristocracy, this freedom does not generally cause large inequalities as would happen if one child were favored to the exclusion of all the others.

The tension between differentialism and universalism makes the Anglo-Saxon relation to strangers and "others" unstable in a way that is unique and fascinating.

Universalist peoples define a priori and forever all outsiders as similar to themselves—an attitude that can lead to some impatience when actual groups of foreigners do not immediately echo back to them their universalist preconception. The xenophobic potential of universalist peoples is evident—one thinks, for example, of the French irritation at the sequestering of Arab women, the contempt of classical Chinese and Romans for those on the peripheries of their empires who did not oppress their women, and the negrophobia of Russians who had little exposure to blacks. Although the opposite anthropological system is never formally and theoretically condemned, peoples of a clearly differentialist persuasion, at least in their conquering phase—such as the Germans and Japanese until the end of World War II—establish stable hierarchical rankings of all peoples of the world from inferior to superior.

In the Anglo-Saxon world, relations can shift as attitudes change. The Anglo-Saxon mind operates with an anthropological borderline, something that does not exist among universalist peoples and that makes the Anglo-Saxon resemble a differentialist people except for the fact that this borderline can be redrawn. It can expand outward or it can pull back. There are "us" and "them" or "brothers and others"—but among all those "others" some are like us and some of them are different. Among those that are "different," some can be reclassified as "like us," and conversely: some of "them" who were considered to be "like us," can be reclassified as "different." But there is always a separation between the completely human and the rest, or, as one says in English, "There is some place where you must draw the line." In the mind of the English, the territory of the human can be reduced to a minimum, i.e., themselves—but it can also extend to all Britons, and today it is certainly in the process of extending to all Europeans.

The history of the United States could be read as the experimental history of this fluctuating borderline, marked first by the continuously expanding inclusive mindset of the central group from its earliest years up until 1965 and subsequently a problematic shrinking from 1965 to the present day.

English in origin, the Americans eventually learned to integrate all Europeans after some significant hesitations in the case of the Irish, Italians, and Jews. The category *white* offered a formal criterion for this partial extension even as it placed "blacks," Indians ("red"), and Asians ("yellow") on the other side of the mental barrier that separates like from unlike. Between 1950 and 1965 there is a new expansion. Asians and North American Indians are redefined as full-fledged Americans—a phenomenon that can be measured by their entry into the general "market" of American marriages. In particular, Asian and Indian women are no longer taboo for the males of the dominant group who are now free to marry them. During the same period the problematic attitude toward blacks becomes the primary focus of tensions over universalism versus differentialism. At the conscious political level the civil rights movement attempts to include blacks within the central space; however, on the unconscious level of deep-seated beliefs their situation hardly changes and the matrimonial segregation of black women decreases only slightly.

The expanding tendency can be explained generously by saying that with time reason has finally proved itself capable of granting the similitude of the other within a conception of a common humanity. This interpretation would imply the existence of an independent egalitarian force that would hold the principle of equality to be intrinsically superior to the principle of inequality. However, if one wants to understand the last and unfortunately temporary expansion of universalism in the United States from 1950 to 1965, the most authentically imperial moment in its history, one has to take into account a second possible explanation—the challenge posed by the Soviet empire. The Cold War period was America's moment of maximum universalism.

Russia invented communism and tried to impose on the world its ideology, certainly the most universalist conception since the French Revolution. The latter offered the principle of liberty to all men. No less egalitarian, the Russian Revolution offered the gulag to all men. No matter what one makes of its other faults, one cannot accuse communism of treating its subject peoples unequally. An examination of the actual functioning of the Soviet empire shows that the state violence and exploitation was more harshly imposed on the Russian center than on the annexed peoples, with the popular democracies of Eastern Europe enjoying a maximum of "liberty," relatively speaking.

The Russian brand of universalism is plain and simple. It could also be very seductive as demonstrated in the meetings of the Communist International. Like the French revolutionaries, the Bolsheviks seem to have had a natural talent for treating all men and peoples in the same way—not just sympathetically but with a sympathy that was favorable for political expansion.

During the Cold War America had to face up to this potential threat that could come from outside or from within. American universalism expressed itself outwardly with the extension to all developed allied countries of a homogeneous liberal economic system and through the encouragement of decolonization throughout the Western sphere of influence. Concurrently, within American society, the challenge raised by communist uni-

versalism made the battle against the segregation of blacks necessary. The world was being asked to choose between two models, and there is no way it could side with an America that treated
a certain group of its citizens as subhuman. The American assimilation of the Japanese and Jews was an undeniable success.
Unlike with these two groups, the political integration of blacks
was not accompanied by an economic emancipation and their
even dispersal throughout American society. A black middle-class
developed, but it has its own ghettos, though fewer in number
than those that group together poor blacks.

Most recently, after the fall of its communist rival, America
shows signs of moving away from universalism. It is as though the
pressure of the rival empire had pushed the United States beyond
what it was really capable of achieving in the area of universalism.
The disappearance of this pressure is permitting the American
psyche to regain its natural equilibrium, which here means
reducing the circumference of the mental circle that will unite
those still to be included within the American "universal."

THE DECLINE OF UNIVERSALISM AT HOME, OR SIGNS OF
INHOSPITALITY TOWARD BLACKS AND HISPANICS

The "multiracial" character of American society and of the statistics that measure that society allow one to follow the internal
weakening of American universalism. Demographic analysis
reveals the failure of black integration and the possible emergence of a third nonintegrated group—the "Hispanic" population, essentially Latin Americans of Indian origin, the overwhelming majority of them Mexicans.

At first glance American census statistics for 2000 show a slight
increase in the number of mixed marriages among black men: 2.3
percent percent among those aged fifty-five and up, and 11 percent among those aged fifteen to twenty-four. But the increase

among black women is near zero, which suggests the persistence of a fundamental racial taboo—the women of the dominated group ought not to marry with the men of the dominant group. Black/white interracial marriage is slightly more common among those who have a college degree. Among Asians, on the other hand, there has been a significant increase in mixed marriages, 8.7 percent and 30.1 percent for the same two older and younger age groups, respectively. Among young Jewish Americans, mixed marriages constitute 50 percent of the total. Interestingly, their entry into the general marriage market, which entails the dissolution of the group, is taking place alongside a vocal increase in active solidarity with the state of Israel.

The most recent statistics, however, reveal that the slight increase in mixed marriages among blacks between 1980 and 1995 has not continued. American census figures allow one to observe the modest liberalizing trend in the years 1980–1995 and the freezing up of the racial situation since then. The percentage of mixed marriages for black women was 1.3 percent in 1980, 1.6 percent in 1990. It went as high as 3.1 percent in 1995 and then receded to 3.0 percent in 1998. But this was no doubt already too much for the statisticians in charge of the *Statistical Abstract of the United States*, who sensed instinctively that this increase, no matter how small, was impossible. For the year 1999 they judiciously separated the statistics for blacks and Hispanics, choosing to place the latter in their own multicolor "Hispanic" category. This made the rate of mixed marriages for black women "drop" to 2.3 percent. So the increase had been a false alarm. A minority population that had inherited Spanish universalist thinking, many of them Puerto Rican no doubt, had been throwing the numbers off with their very large proportion of mixed marriages. Today 98 percent of black women living with a man are living with a black man. If we add to this near total racial endogamy the fact that half of all black women are single mothers and thus by definition not married to a white man, one has to be struck by the remarkable permanence of the racial problem. And not just permanent, but worsening if one considers other regressing demographic indicators.

The rate of infant mortality, defined as the proportion of children dying before age one, is traditionally much higher among blacks than among whites in the United States. In 1997 infant mortality was 6 per 1000 among whites and 14.2 per 1000 among blacks. The rate for white Americans is itself rather mediocre since it is higher than the rate in Japan as well as those in all countries of Western Europe. But at least it is going down. In 1999 it had fallen to 5.8 per 1000. The extraordinary fact is that infant mortality among blacks increased from 14.2 in 1997 to 14.6 in 1999.

Some people may not be accustomed to formulating sociological interpretations on the basis of demographic indicators and might reasonably claim that this increase is small indeed. They might think, moreover, that infant mortality has no general bearing on the society. In fact, the rate of infant mortality is a crucial social yardstick, since it measures the real situation of the most precarious individuals within a given society or of a given sector of that society. In 1976, after observing a small increase in Russian infant mortality between 1970 and 1974, I concluded that the Soviet Union was weakening and I predicted the whole system would soon collapse.[3]

The slight increase in black infant mortality in the United States confirms the failure of racial integration after fifty years of trying.

However, the organization of the American mind at the beginning of this third millennium is not biracial but triracial insofar as statistics and everyday American life have constituted "the Hispanics," in reality Mexicans of Indian origin, as a third specific population group whose numbers are by no means trivial.[4] American society has in effect recreated the three-part structure that existed at the time of independence and later when De Toqueville made his observations at the beginning of the nineteenth century: Indians, blacks, whites.

The destiny of the Mexican community is still a big question mark for sociologists. Certain indicators, such as the excellent acquisition of English among the children, would suggest a continuation of the process of assimilation, the passions of Hispanophobic public debates notwithstanding. However, there has also been a drop, after early increases, in the rate of mixed marriages among younger Hispanics—12.6 percent in the fifty-five-plus age group and 19 percent in the thirty-five to fifty-four age group, but only 17 percent in the twenty-five to thirty-four age group and 15.5 percent in the fifteen to twenty-four age group. This decrease is not necessarily a sign of changing attitudes among Hispanics. It might simply be the natural consequence of the emergence of Mexican majorities within the populations near the Mexican-American border in Texas and California. All the same, this purely territorial effect would indicate a trend toward separation between whites and let us call them Hispano-Indians. The birth rates of the various groups in 1999 is evidence of a persistent division in mental attitudes—1.82 births per woman among non-Hispanic whites (an odd appellation for a racial category!), 2.06 for non-Hispanic blacks, and 2.9 for the Hispanics.[5] In 2001 the birth rate of Mexico was 2.8.

In a society that has replaced the glorification of equal rights with the worship of "diversity"—of origins, cultures, races—known as "multiculturalism," is it really surprising to witness a failure of integration? The retraction of the value of equality in American society is by no means limited to the area of race relations. As we have already seen, the economic evolution from 1980 to 1995 can be described as an accelerated march toward inequality that has led to worsening situations or outright implosion for certain low-income sectors of the population—mostly black as it turns out.

Once again, however, we ought to avoid falling into easy caricatures and try to understand in its totality the mechanism of the Anglo-Saxon mind that needs to segregate some—blacks certainly and maybe Mexicans—in order to assimilate others—the Japanese or Jews, for example. It might be most accurate to speak of a differentialist rather than a universalist assimilation in this case.

In a climate of declining enthusiasm for domestic universalism, the integration of Jews within the mainstream of American society is of particular importance for anyone interested in the strategic choices of the United States. This integration of Jews at home needs to be examined alongside America's movement away from universalism in its foreign policy, in particular in its handling of the Middle East conflict. The inclusion of Israel within the shifting differentialist system of the American mind is taking place both at home and abroad. In the foreign context Arabs are playing the role of excluded "other" that blacks and Mexicans play back in the States.

In the United States the ideological fixation with a Hebrew state is not limited to the Jewish community. The hypothesis of a general movement away from universalism offers a way to understand this fixation. But we ought to examine the history that is currently unfolding with modesty. The solidity of the current links between America and Israel is new and unprecedented. Our purpose here is not to try and explain it so much as it is to use it as another symptom of the basic forces that are currently driving the United States. The partnership with Israel is one of the most visible manifestations of America's move away from universalism and a strengthening of differentialist attitudes that express themselves both abroad with the rejection of Arabs and at home with the integration problems of Mexicans and the persistent segregation of blacks.

THE DECLINE OF UNIVERSALISM ABROAD: CHOOSING ISRAEL

American loyalty toward Israel is truly a mystery for specialists of strategic analysis. A perusal of the recent classic studies offers no explanation. Kissinger treats the Israeli-Palestinian question in detail but with the exasperation of a longtime realist who has to deal with irrational populations fighting for the possession of a promised land. Huntington places Israel outside the sphere of Western civilization that he wants to consider as a strategic bloc.[6] Brzezinski does not discuss Israel, nor does Fukuyama. This is rather odd if one considers the importance of the link with Israel within the establishment of a generalized American antagonism toward the Arab world or, more generally, the Muslim world.

The rationality and purpose of this link are difficult to demonstrate. The hypothesis of necessary cooperation between democracies is unconvincing. The injustice committed day after day toward Palestinians by the Jewish colonization of what remains of their land is itself a negation of the principle of equality that is the foundation of democracy. Other democratic nations, notably those in Europe, do not have the same unconditional sympathy toward Israel that America feels.

The military usefulness of Tsahal, the Israeli army, almost makes more sense as an explanation. The weakness of America's ground forces—so slow and so reluctant to sustain casualties— implies the increasingly systematic use of allied contingents or even mercenaries for carrying out operations on land. Obsessed by the need to control the world's oil supply, American leaders are perhaps unwilling to forego the support of the leading army in the Middle East. With its size and shape and its abundant arms, Israel sits battle ready like an enormous aircraft carrier at anchor amid Arab seas. From the point of view of an American strategic realist, whether civilian or military, to be able to count on a military force capable of eliminating any Arab army within a few days or weeks is more important than the affection or the respect of the Muslim world. But if this is the realist strategy, why do the realist strategists not talk about it? And can one seriously see the Israeli army taking over control of the oil fields of Saudi Arabia, Kuwait, or the United Arab Emirates when one knows that it was formerly unable to control without great loss of life a relatively small piece of southern Lebanon and today cannot maintain control over the West Bank?

Interpretations that insist on the role of the American Jewish community and its capacity to influence electoral politics have a grain of truth. It is the theory of the "Jewish lobby" to which one might add a theory about the nonexistence of an Arab lobby. In the absence of an Arab community sufficiently large to function as a counterweight, the political cost of supporting Israel is near zero for any candidate seeking reelection. Why lose the Jewish vote if there is not a correspondingly larger Arab vote to be won? But we ought not exaggerate the size of the Jewish community, which at 6.5 million constitutes only 2.2 percent of the American population . Moreover, America is not without its traditions of anti-Semitism, and one can imagine that among the 97.8 percent of non-Jewish Americans, there are those who vote against supporters of Israel. But anti-Semites are no longer anti-Israeli. We are now approaching the heart of the mystery.

Groups considered anti-Semitic by American Jews, such as Christian fundamentalists, are politically aligned on the Republican right.[7] But the support for Israel is strongest among right-wing Republicans, and the American religious right that supports Bush has developed a recent passion for the state of Israel—the positive counterpart to its sworn hatred for Islam and the Arab world. If one recalls that on the other side three-quarters of American Jews consider themselves center-left, vote Democrat, and fear the Christian fundamentalists, we arrive at a crucial paradox—American Jews are implicitly antagonistic toward the part of the American electorate that shows the most support for Israel.

One cannot understand the ever more determined support for Ariel Sharon's Israel without taking into account these two rather different sources of support and realizing that their combination and contradictory motivations explain both the continuity and the inconsistencies of American foreign policy toward Israel.

On the one hand there is the traditional support of American Jews. When the Democrats are in power, this support takes the form of attempts to protect Israel while making some effort to respect the rights of Palestinians. The peace process conducted by President Clinton at Camp David is a good example of this kind of support.

Another new and original type of support for Israel originates on the Republican right, which projects onto the context of the Middle East the preference for inequality that characterizes America today. It is not impossible to prefer inequality and injustice after all.

Universalist ideologies proclaim the equivalence of all peoples. This "just" attitude makes those who hold to it also believe it to be necessary for the creation of alliances between peoples. One can, however, form an attachment with someone without any appeal to a notion of equality. During the Peloponnesian War, Athens, the champion of democracies, of course supported the democrats throughout Greece whenever it could. But Sparta, the champion of oligarchies, set up an oligarchical regime whenever it took control of a city.[8] At the end of the eighteenth century, the different European monarchies were able to come together without much difficulty to oppose the principle of equality that had emerged from the French Revolution. The most spectacular example of a distant but firm identification between two regimes that not only opposed equality but embraced the idea of a hierarchy among peoples has to be the alliance between Germany and Japan during World War II. After Pearl Harbor, Hitler declared war on the United States out of solidarity with Japan. Thus there can be a shared preference between countries, just as there can be between individuals, for evil or simple injustice—if, that is, one is evil or unjust oneself. The fundamental principle of identification with someone else is not the recognition of good but the recognition of oneself—good or bad—in the other.

It is in terms of this kind of problematic identification, I believe, that the newly reinforced affection of the United States for Israel needs to be understood. Because Israel is becoming less virtuous at the same time as America, the latter approves of Israel's increasingly ferocious behavior toward the Palestinians. America is sliding toward a firmer belief in the inequality of men and believes less and less in the unity of the human species. These same conditions apply, point by point, to the state of Israel whose policies with regard to Arabs are consistent with its internal social fragmentation as witnessed by its economic inequality and widely divergent religious beliefs. The growing inability of the Israelis to consider Arabs as at bottom human beings like them is evident to anyone who reads a newspaper or watches television. But it is not so easy to observe the process of internal fragmentation of Israeli society that, as in American society, has succumbed to a fever of inegalitarianism.[9] The income gaps between rich and poor are now among the largest of all developed and "democratic" countries. The different Israeli subpopulations—secular, Ashkenazi, Sephardic, and ultra-Orthodox—remain separate as can be seen from the range of birth rates among the different groups that go from two children per woman among secular Israelis to seven for the ultra-Orthodox.

The early relations between Israel and the United States were based on their shared conviction of belonging to a common sphere of liberal democracies. There was also the concrete link of the physical presence on American soil of the largest contingent of Jews from the Diaspora, as well as the biblical link between Calvinism and Judaism. When a Protestant read the Bible in a somewhat literal way, he identified with the people of Israel. In the specific case of American Puritans of the seventeenth century, you have a people who arrive in a promised land exhibiting a horror of idolaters—Indians and blacks—and thereby extending the differentialism of the Bible.

The recent general fixation of the United States on Israel does not seem to have much to do with this original religious affinity,

a love for the Bible, or with a positive and optimistic identification with the chosen people of Israel. I am convinced that if
republican or Catholic France were still at war with Algeria—
repressing, interning, and killing Arabs as the state of Israel is
doing in Palestine—today's United States, differentialist, inegali-
tiarian, and wracked by its own bad conscience—would side with
this colonial France that had abandoned its universalism. There
is nothing more reassuring for those who have given up on justice
than to see others behaving unjustly. The injustice that has lately
taken hold in Israel apparently does not shock today's dominant
Western power.[10]

The most important task of global strategic analysis is to grasp
the deep logic of American behavior. The incapacity of the
United States to see Arabs as other human beings is consistent
with the ebbing of universalism within American society.

WHAT AMERICAN JEWS WORRY ABOUT

This model allows one to understand the nervousness among
American Jews, a community that we might expect to be simply
happy to have successfully accomplished their social integration
and enthusiastically grateful for America's steadfast loyalty toward
Israel. But in fact this privileged community has fallen into the
disturbing, not to say neurotic, cult of the Holocaust.[11] The American Jewish community is endlessly commemorating and "testi-
fying" about the massacre that its members managed to escape. It
endlessly denounces rising anti-Semitism throughout the world
and harbors fears on behalf of all groups of the Diaspora, notably
the French—fears that these individuals themselves do not have
in anywhere near the same degree even though there were, for
example, attacks against synagogues in some quarters of France
in the spring of 2002. French Ashkenazi Jews, for whom the Holocaust was a more concrete family reality than for many American

Jews, seem to be truly less uptight and more confident about the future even if they are perennially derided in America as deserters with no community spirit and as future victims whenever the undying French Judeophobia next rears its ugly head. This persistent Jewish fear in the country with the supposedly all-powerful "Jewish lobby" has something paradoxical about it.[12] The hypothesis of a general ebbing of universalism in America would explain the persistence of Jewish anxiety—*What if my integration is revoked?*

Let us summarize again the key points of our argument. The Anglo-Saxon mind has two characteristics when it comes to its relations with "others." First, it needs to exclude in order to include. Second, the borderline between the included and the excluded is not stable. It waxes and wanes like the moon but without the moon's regularity.

The inclusive integration of American Jews coincides with the exclusion of blacks and maybe Mexicans. Therefore, it has taken place at a time that has seen the general waning of universalism and the slick progress of differentialism via an updated array of American affirmations of "diversity," "difference," and other tribal sentiments. The motor that moves America today is not equality but inequality. So how can one live safe and secure with a clean conscience, given such a twisted process of so-called integration? How can one not experience this "integration" as precarious and subject to who knows what hidden dangers? American Jews project onto the outside world a fear that is much closer to home. They have a vague sense that they may be mere toys or tokens within a regressive differentialist dynamic rather than true beneficiaries of a conquering generosity of a universalist type.

The views I have expressed are not simply the fruits of theoretical reflection. I was enlightened on this subject for the first time in the early 1980s during a conversation with one of my grandfathers, an American of Jewish-Austrian origin. On a visit to Disneyland, as Mickey and his friends danced about us, he told me of his nagging anxiety—the racial passion in American society reminded him unpleasantly of the Vienna of his adolescence. I have never observed this kind of nervousness on the Jewish-French side of my family.

AN EMPIRE CANNOT BE DIFFERENTIALIST

The American rhetoric about an "evil empire," an "axis of evil," or any other earthly manifestations of the devil's handiwork is so grossly inept that one has to smile and shake one's head or else scream in outrage depending on the moment and one's personal temperament. However, it ought to be taken seriously in its decoded form. This rhetoric truthfully expresses an American obsession with evil that is identified accusingly as emanating from outside the country when in fact it originates from inside the United States. The menace of evil in the United States is truly everywhere if one thinks of the renunciation of the principle of equality, the rise of an irresponsible plutocracy, the overdrawn credit card existence of millions of consumers and the country as a whole, the increasing use of the death penalty, and the return with a vengeance of obsessions about race. Not to mention the disturbing anthrax episodes post-9/11 that may have been carried out by demented and unsupervised members of the secret service. God has certainly not been blessing America lately. The country is steaming mad about the evil it sees everywhere, no doubt in part because the kettle cannot see how black it has become. This regression can make us more aware of what we are all losing, namely the America of 1950–1965, a broadly democratic country where freedom of speech, an expansion of social programs, and the fight for civil rights made it an empire of good in spite of the mistakes derived from the Anything But Communism policies exemplified by McCarthyism.

So-called American unilateralism—the term itself is a striking irruption of differentialist thinking in international politics—will not be considered in this study from an essentially moral angle. One must look at its causes and practical consequences. The fundamental cause, as we have seen, is a move away from caring about equality and universalism in the United States itself. The fundamental consequence is America's loss of an indispensable resource of all empires. Without a homogeneous vision of a united humanity composed of its many peoples, America will not be able to reign over such a vast and diverse world. An ideal of justice was an arm in the arsenal of its "soft power" that America no longer possesses. The post—World War II period from 1950–1965, while far from perfect, was the high-water mark for American universalism. As with the universalism of imperial Rome, America triumphed briefly through modesty and generosity.

The Romans knew to appreciate the superiority of Greek philosophy, mathematics, literature, and fine arts. The Roman aristocracy Hellenized itself. The winner on the battlefield adopted many of the characteristics of the superior culture of the defeated country. Rome allowed itself to be influenced by several Middle Eastern religions before deciding to focus on one only. During its authentically imperial moment, the United States was curious and respectful toward the outside world. Americans observed and analysed sympathetically the diversity of the world's societies via political science, anthropology, literature, and cinema. Preserving the best of what it finds in the world is the mark of the true universalist empire. The conqueror's force permits cultures to fuse. This time in American history that combined military and economic strength with intellectual and cultural tolerance now seems far away. The weakened and nonproductive post-Y2K America is no longer tolerant or confident. It pretends to incarnate an exclusive human ideal, to know all the secrets of economic success, and to produce the only movies worth watching. The recent boasting about its presumed social and cultural hegemony, the progress of its ever expanding narcissism, is only one of the many

6

Confront the Strong or Attack the Weak?

The movement of American society and its economy toward inequality and especially inefficiency has ended up reversing the relation of the United States to the rest of the world. After being an extraordinary superpower in the fall of 1945, America has become a sort of black hole—absorbing merchandise and capital but incapable of furnishing the same goods in return. To assure its hold over the world that nourishes it, the country has to define a new role for itself other than the one it has lately fallen into, namely that of being the world's ultimate Keynesian consumer. This is not easy. Its redefinition as a hegemonic power has to be a political and military imposition—it must put itself forward as *the* state of the entire planet and acquire a global monopoly on legitimate domination. However, America does not have the necessary resources for this sort of recasting of itself—neither in terms of *hard power* nor of *soft power*, to use the favorite concepts of Joseph Nye.

Free trade, as we have seen, introduces problems for growth on a global scale and is now a brake on the prosperity of the world. In the short term it allows America to carry on by means of mechanisms that can only be called baroque. The slowdown in demand caused by free trade puts the United States in the position of an overweight, hamstrung designated consumer. Meanwhile the rise of inequality that is another consequence of the system allows for the bulimia of profits that go to the United States in the form of fresh capital that is then used to finance its consumption.

America's position as the central regulator is precarious, as we have seen, because the collection of imperial tribute does not happen in an authoritarian manner but instead via a "liberal," voluntary mechanism that is subtle, instable, and terribly dependent on the goodwill of the ruling classes that live in the dominated periphery — particularly Europeans and the Japanese. One can accuse Wall Street and American banks of any number of confidence games, but one cannot accuse them of forcing their users and clients to throw their money at them . . . away.

The deregulated form of capitalism that the United States champions has steadily lost its legitimacy, to the point where the January-February 2002 issue of the journal *Foreign Affairs* begins with a study of the strategic threat posed by resistance to globalization.

The insufficiency of America's power to impose its will militarily complicates the economic problem. Although undeniably superior in the air and on the sea, American ground forces cannot directly control the geographic area that produces the vital merchandise and amasses the financial sums necessary for America's day-to-day existence. More important, the airpower that in theory would suffice for establishing absolute power, through the threat of bombardments, cannot operate with a free hand given the continued existence of the only power whose antiaircraft capability could neutralize, partially or totally, the U.S. Air Force, namely Russia. So long as the latter exists, America does not have the total power that could sustain long-term economic security in the new role it must play as the world's dependent rentier.

Besides economic dependence and an inadequate military, a third key element must be added to this outline of American deficiencies, namely the ebbing of a universalist sentiment that will prevent the United States from forming an egalitarian, just, and responsible vision of the planet. Universalism is a fundamental resource for any state, whether it seeks to dominate and rule over a nation or over a more vast, multiethnic, and imperial domain.

These three explanatory elements expose the fundamental contradiction of America's position in the world. The United States has to institute a stable and durable imperial economic equilibrium without really having the military and ideological means to do it. In order to fully understand American foreign policy, however, we ought to examine further the way in which this fundamental contradiction got started by describing the path that led to this awkward position that is half imperial and half liberal. Nothing amid the succession of decisions that have led to the present dilemma would seem to indicate the existence of a deliberate long-term project.

The imperial option is recent. It is not the result of a strongly willed plan but instead presented itself to American leaders as the easy way out. It is a product of circumstances. The collapse of the Soviet system, while offering the momentary illusion of absolute power, led to the dream of establishing a stable, global hegemony in two phases. But 1995 rather than 1990 was the decisive moment.

FROM THE FALL OF COMMUNISM TO THE FALL OF RUSSIA

Soviet leaders and American strategists did not foresee the collapse of the Soviet system, the communist rival that competed with the "Free World" in the aftermath of World War II and gave the liberal sphere a kind of negative coherence as "noncommunist." At the beginning of the 1990s, in fact, the United States was engaged in thinking about its own economic deficiencies. In *The Competitive Advantage of Nations* (1990), Michael Porter described how different capitalist systems—Japanese, German, Swedish, Korean—were outperforming the Anglo-Saxon model in production because they only accepted the liberal rules when it was to their advantage to do so.[1]

One of the early consequences of the fall of communism, and with it the disappearance of the principal enemy, seems to have been a foregrounding of the rivalry between the United States and the leading European and Asian capitalist powers. In *Head to Head* (1993), Lester Thurow announced the future economic war between the United States, Europe, and Japan.[2] We must remember that at this stage the American government, like all others, had barely begun to digest the surprising fall of communism and was thus equally unprepared for the dissolution of Russia as a superpower. After having overestimated the economic health of communism, the industrialized world underestimated the difficulties associated with unplugging from communism.

At the start of the 1990s the most probable hypothesis by all accounts held that there would be a continuation of a substantial Russian strategic position in a world no longer defined by an ideological polarization but still containing two superpowers. It was possible to dream of an egalitarian and balanced world where all nations would be playing by the same rules. In this context the United States went along with the idea of a return to an equilibrium between nations. Its moves toward disarmament, as we have noted, were numerous and highly visible. There were no signs at that time of any wish to exercise the imperial option. But between 1990 and 1995 the breakdown of the former Soviet bloc became apparent and the economic implosion of its various republics truly dramatic.

Russian production dropped by 50 percent between 1990 and 1995. Investment shrunk to nothing. The use of the currency became undependable to the point where in some areas there was a return to systems of barter. The independence of Ukraine, Belarus, and Kazakstan—the latter ethnically half Russian—cut 75 million people out of the "slavic" heart of the former Soviet system. As a result, Russia was no longer the rough demographic equivalent of the United States. In 1981 the population of the Soviet Union was 268 million compared to America's 230 million. By 2001 Russia's population had fallen to 144 million. America's had grown to 285 million.

Worse still, national and ethnic independence movements were not confined to the former Soviet republics but also became commonplace in the autonomous regions within the Russian Federation from the Caucasus to Tartarstan. The central administration also seemed to have lost control over the distant Siberian regions. There was speculation about a breakup of the purely Russian regions themselves—the dissolution of the Russian state into a bunch of feudal fragments.[3] Many signs pointed to the possibility of total disintegration. Around 1996 America's old strategic adversary seemed on the verge of simply disappearing. It was at this moment that the imperial option occurred to the United States, mostly because the possibility of an imbalanced world dominated militarily by the United States seemed possible or even probable. With a little pushing and shoving by the United States on the edges of the Russian Federation, notably in the Caucasus and in Central Asia, its two soft spots, it could have been checkmate and winner take all. Not surprisingly, Brzezinski's *The Grand Chessboard* appeared in 1997 and would be regarded by some as the most coherent strategy manual for describing the necessity and the means for establishing asymmetrical American domination over Eurasia.

The fall of Russia left the United States as the only military superpower. Alongside these developments the globalization of investment accelerated. In the seven years from 1990 to 1997 the positive balance of capital movements between America and the rest of the world went from 60 billion to 271 billion dollars. The United States was then able to indulge in large amounts of conspicuous consumption without worrying about paying for it out of its own production.

The idea of an imperial option should not, however, lead us to imagine a circle of clairvoyant and calculating American leaders shrewdly deciding on the right moment to spring its masterplan on the world and then consistently carry it out. On the contrary, the adoption of the imperial option was characterized by a general abandonment to the flow of time and tide and a constant preference for whatever seemed easiest. The American ruling class is even more rudderless and clueless than its European counterparts who are so often criticized for their weakness. After all, the ongoing construction of Europe requires making concerted efforts to organize and cooperate in ways that the current American leadership is wholly incapable of.

Choosing to remain a leading nation rather than become an empire would have been by far the better long-term strategy for the United States. Moreover, it would have been far easier to achieve in America given the continental proportions of the country and the centrality of its investment system. But it would have required a lot of organizational and regulatory hard work on the part of the administration. Most important, it would have necessitated an energy policy combined with a protectionist economic policy to defend industry. At the same time, this two-pronged domestic policy would have had as an external counterpart a multilateral foreign policy to encourage other nations and regions to move toward economic autonomy beneficial to all. Reinvigorating developed economies on a regionalist basis would have permitted offering practical help to developing countries in the form of debt forgiveness in exchange for the return of protectionism. A worldwide plan of this sort would have made the United States the world's undeniable and definitive leader. But thinking it all up and putting it into action would have been so tiring.

It was much easier and more self-gratifying to await the final collapse of Russia and the emergence of the United States as the unique superpower, welcome the flood of incoming capital, and float merrily along into deeper and deeper trade deficits. While justifying itself with the liberal ideology of laissez-faire, the imperial option was most certainly, and especially psychologically, the outcome of a bumbling, willy-nilly attitude. This non-strategy-turned-strategy, long on ambition but short on motivation, turned on a key unknown variable—one could not be sure in 1997 if Russia was definitively out of the picture. Any U.S. foreign policy that took as a given something that was still so uncertain would force the country to take an enormous risk. If Russia were not to die, America could find itself one day in the embarrassing situation of being deeply dependent economically but without the real military superiority to make up for it. In short, it risked going from being a semi-imperial power to becoming a pseudoimperial power.

If it had been thought through properly and were the result of a strong will, the diplomatic and military strategy appropriate to the imperial option would at least have been applied consistently and methodically. This did not happen. To demonstrate the absence of a clear consistent effort in this regard, the easiest thing is to analyze the very blunt imperial strategy put forward by Brzezinski and ask whether the Americans were able to stick to it. An examination of recent history reveals that they were able to do all the easy parts in an off-the-cuff manner and gave up in all those areas that would have required large investments of time and energy.

THE GRAND CHESSBOARD OF DIPLOMACY

Brzezinski's plan is clear and concise, even if he suggests that wiping out Russia is for its own good. He proposes bringing Ukraine into the occidental fold and using Uzbekistan to pry Central Asia out of Russia's control. He does not say that encircling Russia need necessarily lead to the breakup of the heart of the country. His high strategy does not forego a minimum of diplomatic caution. But there are things even more unspeakable. Brzezinski does not broach the subject of America's economic inefficiency and the necessity for the United States to insure control over the world's wealth through political and military means. However, his geopolitical experience does lead him to formulate this vital matter indirectly, first by underlining the fact that the bulk of the world's population is in Eurasia, and second by pointing out that the United States is a long way away from Eurasia. Read: Eurasia supplies the influx of goods and capital that are indispensable for maintaining the standard of living of all Americans, from the overclass to the plebeians.

All reservations aside, the plan is coherent enough. The only obstacle to building an American empire is Russia, so it ought to be isolated and picked apart. One might call this the Bismarck approach to U.S. problems, in which Russia would be playing the role of France in the years 1871–1890. Back then Chancellor Bismarck managed to create a united German nation by trouncing France in 1870–71. During the next twenty years he worked to maintain good relations with all the other European powers in order to isolate France as their sole adversary and stigmatize it as eternally scheming to take revenge for the loss of Alsace and Lorraine. Brzezinski recommends that the United States take a conciliatory line with all nations except Russia. Having understood perfectly well that true U.S. control over Eurasia depends above all on the consent of the European and Japanese protectorates, he advises the United States to solidify its hold on Eurasia by allowing Japan to take on greater global stature beyond its Asian role and by adopting an understanding attitude toward the construction project of Europe. Curiously, only England is treated condescendingly by Brzezinski and considered a nonentity. The

French-German tandem is respected as a major strategic player. And in what must be considered the height of political savvy, Brzezinski even suggests a more understanding attitude toward France. The initial idea is perfectly lucid: so long as Europe and Japan are satisfied with American leadership, the empire is invulnerable. It would then coalesce within itself the most substantial share of technological and economic power in the world. Beyond this core strategy, Brzezinski also recommends a conciliatory attitude toward China, a country whose future status as potential rival is still a long way off, and Iran, a country whose likely evolution will not lead to confrontation. Squeezed between Europe and Japan, cut off from China and Iran, Russia would effectively be deprived of all means of maneuvering in Eurasia. To summarize, America, the only superpower, had to be understanding toward all secondary powers in order to definitively eliminate Russia, the only immediate military threat to American hegemony.

What part of this program was effectively pursued by American diplomacy? Really only the action of provoking Russia with the eastward expansion of NATO, with some overtures to Ukraine, and with seizing all possible pretexts for extending America's influence in the Caucasus region and Central Asia. The war against Al Qaeda and the Taliban regime allowed the United States to station twelve thousand of its soldiers in Afghanistan, fifteen hundred in Uzbekistan, and a hundred or so in Georgia. But in these instances the American government was content to take advantage of circumstances. As we shall see in the next chapter, the effort is weak and not enough to decisively destabilize Russia, something America no longer has the means to do.

When it comes to the rest of the plan, one would have to say that instead of following the brilliant Bismarck, the American diplomatic corps looks more like the reckless Wilhelm II. Once he had gotten rid of Bismarck, Wilhelm II rushed to provoke conflicts with two major European powers, Great Britain and Russia, and in effect gave France the keys for opening alliances that would lead directly to World War I and the end of German hegemony. In similar fashion America is being neglectful by humiliating its European allies with its unilateral action and by allowing NATO, an essential part of its power, to drift aimlessly. It criticizes Japan, a country whose economy is highly efficient and essential to the health of the United States, with endless claims of how it is behind the curve. It never tires of provoking China and has seen fit to include Iran within the "axis of evil." From the looks of it, one might think that America was trying to create a Eurasian coalition of very different countries by uniting them around their shared annoyance over its erratic behavior. We can also mention as part of that behavior, though it goes somewhat beyond the strategic contours that most interest Brzezinski, the obstinacy with which the United States has managed to generalize its conflict with the Muslim world through its unflinching support of Israel.

But America's clumsy tactlessness is not something out of the blue. Like the imperial option, it is the result of being lazily carried along, on the one hand, and short-term necessities, on the other. The limited military, economic, and ideological resources of the United States leave it no other way of affirming its global importance than by mistreating minor powers. There is a hidden logic behind the drunken sailor appearance of American diplomacy. The real America is too weak to take on anyone except military midgets. By provoking all of these secondary players, it can at least affirm its global role. Being economically dependent on the rest of the world, it will have a global presence of one kind or another. The insufficiency of its real resources is leading to a hysterical dramatization of second-order conflicts. Moreover, the weakening of its universalist sensibility has made it forget that if it wants to continue to rule, it must treat equally and fairly its principal allies, Europe and Japan, who together dominate world industry.

THE BIG LITTLE BULLY

The stubborn determination of the United States to cultivate a seemingly pointless hostility toward such outdated remains of a bygone era as North Korea, Cuba, and Iraq shows every sign of the most perfect irrationality. Even more so if one considers its distemper with regard to Iran, a nation clearly on the road to becoming a normal democracy, and its frequent provocations of China. A genuinely imperial attitude would want to lay the groundwork for a Pax Americana by, among other things, exhibiting a patient indulgence toward countries whose current status is so clearly temporary. The North Korean, Cuban, and Iraqi regimes would tumble with no outside intervention. One can already see Iran changing for the better. Yet it is perfectly clear that American aggression makes absurd communist regimes dig in their heels, blocks change within the Iraqi regime, and gives credence to the anti-American sentiments of Iran's conservatives. In China, where the communist leaders are conducting an authoritarian transition toward capitalism, American hostility has the effect of continually offering a legitimating alibi for the regime's exploitation of nationalist fervor and xenophobia. A new area of operations has recently been opened up by America the arsonist-fireman, namely in the conflict between India and Pakistan. Though largely responsible for Pakistan's political instability and locally virulent Islamism, the United States has no qualms about volunteering its services as the indispensable mediator of those conflicts.

All of this is bad for the world and annoys American allies, but it is anything but nonsensical. These conflicts that represent little or no military risk allow the United States to be "present" throughout the world. The United States works to maintain the illusory fiction of the world as a dangerous place in need of America's protection.

The first war on Iraq led by Bush I furnished the blueprint that now dominates American foreign policy. One hardly dare speak anymore of a strategy because the very short-term rationalizations of America are likely to provoke a radical weakening of its position in the world in the near future.

What is Iraq? An oil-soaked country run by a dictator with only a local capacity for making trouble. The circumstances of Iraqi aggression against Kuwait are obscure, and we are sill far from knowing if the United States may not have intentionally provoked Saddam Hussein's transgression by letting him understand that an annexation of Kuwait was not unacceptable in America's view. But that question is of secondary importance. What is certain is that the liberation of Kuwait gave shape to a convenient option: engage in a maximum number of conflicts against two-bit military opponents that will first be blackballed as "rogue states"—a quaint name that recalls the fictional, Manichean worlds of Falstaff, Dickens, and Mark Twain—and then whipped soundly so as to "demonstrate" the force of America. The opponent has to be weak. Notice that Vietnam, still a communist country and still America's symbol of real military capacity—and justifiably so—has not been picked on. The exaggeration of the Iraqi threat—the fourth largest army in the world we are told!—will be remembered as only the first act in America's dramatic staging of nonexistent global dangers that the United States will rush to save us from.

The war in Afghanistan that followed the attacks of September 11 confirmed this option. Yet again American leaders got the country involved in a conflict that they had not foreseen but that served the purposes of their modus operandi that we could name "theatrical micromilitarism": demonstrate the necessity of America in the world by slowly annihilating insignificant adversaries. In the case of Afghanistan, the demonstration was less than perfect. It certainly did show the world that no country without an effective antiaircraft capability or a nuclear deterrent would be safe from the horrors of aerial bombardments. But the inability of the American army to impose itself on the ground in Afghanistan recalled a fundamental weakness of this superpower and revealed its dependence not just on local tribal chiefs but on the goodwill of the Russians who were in the area and the only force capable of furnishing arms to the Northern Alliance. End result: neither the Mullah Omar nor Bin Laden was captured. Instead, the local chiefs handed over a few miserable low-ranking functionaries to their American employer. These insignificant prisoners were locked up on the island military base of Guantanamo in Cuba, a country whose leader, Fidel Castro, has nothing in common with these fundamentalists besides a shared fondness for beards. Thus out of whole cloth, or beards in this case, a fictive relation is invented between the "Cuban problem" and the "war on terrorism" symbolized by Al Qaeda and the Taliban. Building up the idea of an "axis of evil" with the help of the media is an American policy objective.

THE OBSESSION WITH ISLAM

The distribution of American forces in the world reveals the true state of the empire, or of its remains if one believes that it is falling apart rather than gaining in strength. Germany, Japan, and South Korea are still the three places with the highest number of American troops outside the United States. The creation of military bases in Hungary, Bosnia, Afghanistan, and Uzbekistan since 1990 has not significantly altered this overall picture that dates from the days of the war on communism. The only remaining declared enemies from this former time are Cuba and North Korea. These puny states are endlessly criticized, but the harsh language has never been followed up by the least military action.

The bulk of American military activities is now directed at the Muslim world as part of a "war on terrorism"—the latest official marquee of its micromilitary theater. Three factors explain the American obsession with this religion, which happens also to be a region. Each factor corresponds to one of the deficiencies—ideological, economic, military—of the United States when it comes to imperial resources. The ideological move away from universalist ideology has led to a new intolerance with regard to the status of women in the Muslim world. The decline in economic performance has led to an obsession with Arab oil. The weakness of the American military has made the Muslim world, itself known for being extremely deficient militarily, an easy target.

ANGLO-SAXON FEMINISM AND CONTEMPT
FOR THE ARAB WORLD

As it becomes increasingly intolerant of the diversity in the world, America spontaneously sees an antagonist in the Arab world. The objections to it are visceral, primitive, and deeply anthropological. It goes way beyond the religious differences used by Huntington to position the Muslim world outside the Western sphere. An anthropologist used to working on social customs can see that the Anglo-Saxon and Arab systems have been pushed to opposite extremes.

The American family is nuclear, individualist, and reserves a high place for women as wives and mothers. The Arab family is extended, patrilinear, and places women in a situation of maximum dependence. Marriage between first cousins is particularly taboo in the Anglo-Saxon world but preferred in the Arab world. In the United States, feminism has become over the years increasingly dogmatic and aggressive, and genuine tolerance for the real diversity in the world is forever waning. Thus it was in a sense destined to come into conflict with the Arab world and the rest of the Muslim world where family structures resemble those in the Arab world. This would include Pakistan, Iran, and part of

Turkey, but not Indonesia, Malaysia, or the Islamic peoples of Africa along the Indian Ocean where the status of women is high.

The conflict between America and the Arab-Muslim world has the unpleasant appearance of a deep-seated anthropological divide, an unarguable confrontation between opposing sets of first principles. There is something worrisome about seeing this kind of difference become a defining force in international relations. Since September 11 this cultural conflict has taken on a buffoonish quality that could be characterized as global street theater. On one side America, the country of castrating women, where the former president had to prove to authorities that he did not have sexual relations with a White House intern; on the other Bin Laden, a polygamous terrorist with countless half-brothers and half-sisters. Taken together, we have a caricature of a world that is fast disappearing. The Muslim world does not need America's advice when it comes to improving its social customs.

The fall in birth rates in most of the Muslim countries itself implies an improving situation for women. First, because it means at the same time higher literacy rates, and second, it means that a country such as Iran, where a rate of 2.1 births per woman has been attained, must necessarily contain a large number of families who have given up on having one or more sons and who have thus broken with the patrilineal tradition.[4] In the case of Egypt, one of the few countries for which regular statistics about marriage between cousins is available, there has been a decrease from 25 percent in 1992 to 22 percent in 2000.

During the war in Afghanistan there emerged a parallel discourse of cultural war demanding an improved status for Afghan women. This discourse was moderate in Europe but conducted at very high volume in the Anglo-Saxon world. We were practically being told that U.S. planes were bombing Islamic antifeminism. This kind of Western demand is ridiculous. Customs do evolve, but it is a slow process that a modern war pursued blindly can only slow down — because the feminist leaning Western civilization gets associated with unarguable military ferocity and thus, by contrast, gives an absurd nobility to the hypermasculinist ethic of the Afghan warlords.

The conflict between the Anglo-Saxon world and the Arab-Muslim world runs deep. And there are worse sides to it than the feminist views of Mrs. Bush and Mrs. Blair toward Afghan women. Anglo-Saxon social and cultural anthropology shows some signs of degeneration. After efforts to comprehend the lives of individuals living in different systems, as in the exemplary work of Evans-Pritchard and Meyer Fortes, we have seen ignorant suffragettes denouncing masculine dominance in New Guinea or, in the opposite case, openly expressing praise for the matrilineal systems on the coast of Tanzania and Mozambique that also happen to have Muslim majorities. If social scientists begin handing out good and bad report cards to different peoples, what hope is there for expecting a dispassionate approach on the part of governments and armies?

As we have already noted, "universalism" does not guarantee tolerance. The French, for example, are perfectly capable of being hostile toward Maghreb immigrants because the status of the Arab woman contradicts their social customs. But the reaction is instinctive and includes no ideological formalization, no overall judgment about the Arab anthropological system. Universalism is a priori blind to difference and cannot lead to the condemnation of this or that system. The "war on terrorism," on the other hand, has given rise to all kinds of definitive categorical judgments about the Afghan or Arab systems that are incompatible with an egalitarian predisposition. My point is that these pronouncements are not just random anecdotes but the symptoms of the decline of universalism in the Anglo-Saxon world, a decline that prevents the United States from having an uncorrupted vision of international relations and in particular from being able to deal decently and strategically well with the Muslim world.

ECONOMIC DEPENDENCE AND THE OBSESSION WITH OIL

The American oil policy, naturally focused on the Middle East, is a result of the new economic relationship between the United States and the world. Historically the leader in discovering, refining, and using crude oil, the United States has become a huge importer of oil in the last thirty years. If one compares its situation to that of Europe and Japan, where production is low or nonexistent, it has in a sense become like everyone else.

In 1973 the United States pumped 9.2 million barrels a day and imported 3.2 million. In 1999 it was producing 5.9 million per day and importing 8.6. At current levels of consumption, American oil reserves will be used up in 2010. It is easy to understand the American obsession with oil and the proportionately high number of oilmen in the Bush administration. The fixation of the United States on this energy resource is not, however, completely rational or indicative of an effective imperial strategy, and this for several reasons.

First, because, given the overall dependence on imports of the U.S. economy, singling out oil for special attention is more symbolic than anything else. An America well supplied with oil but lacking its accustomed supply of other imported goods would experience the same shock to its standard of living as an America deprived of oil. As we have seen, oil imports represent a sizeable but still secondary portion of the American trade deficit—80 billion of the 450 billion dollars for the year 2000. In fact, America would be vulnerable in the event of an interruption of just about anything, so the centrality of the oil question has no rational economic explanation.

Second, fear of an interruption of oil supplies should in no way lead to an obsession with the Middle East. The countries that supply America's energy needs are spread pretty much all over the globe. Despite its dominant role as a producer and its large percentage of global reserves, the Arab world in no way holds the United States over a barrel, so to speak. Half of American petroleum imports come from countries in the New World that pose no military threat to the United States—principally Mexico, Canada, and Venezuela. Total imports from these countries plus the domestic American production accounts for 70 percent of U.S. consumption, with only 30 percent coming from sources outside the sphere of American influence defined in the Monroe Doctrine. Compared with Europe and Japan that really do depend on the Middle East, the United States enjoys a high degree of oil security. The oil from countries along the Persian Gulf, for example, represents only 18 percent of American consumption. The presence of America's navy and air force in the region, its ground forces in Saudi Arabia, its diplomatic battles with Iran, and its repeated attacks against Iraq are certainly elements within an overall oil strategy. The energy supply it seeks to control, however, is not America's but the world's, and in particular the supply of the two poles that are both industrially productive and overwhelming exporters to the United States—Europe and Japan. Here the American foreign policy could indeed be described as imperial, and this is not necessarily a comforting thought.

At present, the large populations and undiversified economies in Iran, Iraq, and even Saudi Arabia give these countries no choice but to sell their oil. Therefore, Europeans and Japanese have nothing to fear, given the very limited autonomy of these nations. The United States pretends to be guaranteeing the allies' oil supply. The truth of the matter is that by controlling the energy needs of Europe and Japan, the United States believes it reserves the right to exert significant pressure on them if necessary.

The picture I have painted here should be thought of as the fantasy of an aging strategist à la Donald Rumsfeld who has at hand a few numbers and few maps. The reality is that the United States has lost control of Iran and that Saudi Arabia is in the process of slipping out of its hands. The American push to estab-

TABLE 9. American Oil Imports in 2001
(in Millions of Barrels)

Total	3,475
Algeria	3
Egypt	2.5
Iraq	285
Iran	0
Kuwait	88
Oman	6
Qatar	0
Saudi Arabia	585
United Arab Emirates	5
Angola	122
Brunei	2
China	5
Congo (Brazzaville)	16
Congo (Kinshasa)	5
Indonesia	15
Malaysia	5
Nigeria	309
Dutch Antilles	6
Canada	485
Ecuador	43
Mexico	498
Peru	2.5
Trinidad-Tobago	19
Venezuela	520
Other	453

SOURCE: http://www.census.gov/foreign-trade

lish permanent military bases in Saudi Arabia after the Gulf War can be viewed as a last ditch effort to avoid losing control over the whole region. This ebbing control is the underlying strategic reality. No armada of aircraft carriers so far from the United States can maintain military supremacy without the cooperation of at least some local countries. The Saudi and Turkish military bases are technically more important than American aircraft carriers.

The American fixation on the oil of the Muslim world has more to do with fears of being kicked out of the region than with designs to expand its empire. It says more about the worries of the United States than about its power—first, a worry over the all too real prospect of overall economic dependence for which the energy deficit is only a fitting symbol, and second, a worry over the prospect of losing control over its two productive protectorates, Europe and Japan.

SHORT-TERM SOLUTION: ATTACK THE WEAK

Beyond all apparent American motives—indignation over the status of Arab women or the importance of oil—the choice of the Muslim world as the target and privileged pretext of America's theatrical militarism, whose real object is to illustrate at low-cost the strategic omnipotence of the United States, follows quite simply from the overall weakness of the Arab world. It is by its nature the sacrificial lamb. As Huntington notes—sadly or gladly, one cannot easily tell—Muslim civilization has no dominant central state or "core state" as he terms it. It is true that in the Arab-Muslim sphere there is no powerful state in terms of population, industry, and military capacity. Neither Egypt, Saudi Arabia, Pakistan, Iraq, nor Iran has the material and human resources to mount a true resistance. Israel, moreover, has demonstrated on several occasions the present-day military ineffectiveness of the Arab countries. Their current levels of social development and state organization seem for now incompatible with the deployment of an effective military.

The region is thus an ideal staging ground for the United States, since it can rack up "victories" with all the ease of an experienced video game user. The lesson of the defeat in Vietnam was perfectly assimilated by the American military establishment. It recognizes the weakness of its ground forces and never ceases to point out—whether via the slip of the tongue of a general who confuses Afghanistan and Vietnam or the evident fear of putting troops on the ground—that the only type of war possible for the United States is one against a weak adversary with no antiaircraft defenses. There is no doubt, moreover, that by targeting a weak opponent, by choosing asymmetry, the American army has gone back to its old military tradition, consistent with differentialist thinking, which began with the wars against Indians.

Playing the anti-Arab card is an easy answer for the United States. It relates to several objective parameters such as the necessity for the United States to maintain a show of imperial prerogative. But it is not the result of clearly thinking through the central requirements for optimizing the long-term chances of an American empire. On the contrary. America's leaders always let themselves be tempted by the path of least resistance. Every time it is the most immediately easy course of action that is chosen—the one that is the least demanding in terms of economic, military, or even conceptual investment. The United States will mistreat Arabs because they are militarily weak, because they have oil, and because the aura of oil will shift attention away from America's global dependence on merchandise of all sorts. Arabs can also be mistreated because there is no effective Arab lobby on the chessboard of American politics and because the United States is no longer capable of thinking in universalist and egalitarian ways.

If we want to understand what is happening, we must absolutely lay aside the idea of an America acting on the basis of a global plan that has been rationally thought through and methodically applied. American foreign policy has a direction, but it is about as directed as the current of a river. Choosing the path of least resistance also means "choosing" the steepest gradient and eventually the streams join and the river flows into the ocean. Things are no doubt moving but without the least bit of thinking or mastery. This is now the American way—the way of a superpower, there is no question, but one powerless to maintain control over a world that is too big and whose diversity is too strong for it. Each one of the options chosen for its ease is leading to worse difficulties in those areas where it would have been preferable to act instead of react, to temporarily go against the easy flow and the steepest downhill path and instead accept to hike back uphill for a ways. I am talking about rebuilding an industrial base; paying the price of the true loyalty of one's allies by treating their interests with respect; confronting forcefully the true strategic adversary, Russia, rather than simply toying with it; and imposing an equitable peace on the Israeli-Palestinian conflict.

American actions in the Persian Gulf, attacks on Iraq, threats against North Korea, and provocations of China are all part of the American strategy of theatrical micromilitarism. They amuse the media and stun allied leaders. But these gestures divert energy from the major axes of a realist American strategy that should focus on maintaining U.S. control of the industrial poles of Europe and Japan, neutralizing China and Iran with a magnanimous attitude, and definitively breaking up its only real military opponent, Russia. In the two remaining chapters, I plan to show how the return of Russia and the emergent autonomy of Europe and Japan will lead to the breakdown of the American order in the near future. I will also show how the micromilitary agitation of the United States is bringing about closer relations between the major strategic players—Europe, Russia, and Japan. In other words, exactly the opposite of what the United States should be trying to achieve if it really wants to be an empire. The nightmare hidden behind Brzezinski's dream is about to come true—Eurasia is trying to learn to walk without the help of the United States.

7

The Return of Russia

The United States is failing in its attempt to eliminate or simply isolate Russia—even if it continues to act as if its old strategic adversary were no longer a factor, either by humiliation or by affecting the sort of kindness one accords to the old and infirm, and sometimes by combining both attitudes. On his travels through Europe at the end of May 2002, George W. Bush spoke of cooperation with Russia while at the same time American troops were setting up operations in the Caucasus in Georgia. Most of the time Washington takes obvious pleasure in announcing to the world that NATO can be enlarged or an American missile defense system can be started without consulting Moscow. However, to say Russia does not exist is to deny reality, since without its help the American army would not have been able to set foot in Afghanistan. But theatrical micromilitarism requires this posturing—empire must be simulated, especially as America begins to place itself in tactical dependence vis-à-vis Russia.

Faced with the Russia question, the American strategy had two goals—the first is no longer attainable and the second grows less likely over time. The first objective was the disintegration of Russia, something that was supposed to be sped along by stimulating independence movements in the Caucasus and with an American military presence in Central Asia. These demonstrations of force were supposed to encourage the centrifugal tendency of the provinces within the ethnically Russian part of the federation. This policy seriously underestimated Russian national cohesion.

The second objective was to maintain a certain level of tension between the United States and Russia and thereby prevent a reconciliation between Europe and Russia—in other words the reunification of Western Eurasia—by keeping alive for as long as possible the antagonist climate inherited from the Cold War. But the disorder and incertitude engendered by America's Middle East policy has had the opposite effect and has created the optimum conditions for Russia's being dealt back in as an international player, a situation that Vladimir Putin has taken advantage of immediately. In an impressive speech, given mostly in German before the Bundestag on September 23, 2001, Putin offered the West a true end to the Cold War. But what West? Offering short-term help to the Americans in their made-for-TV micromilitary show in Afghanistan—the traditional object of a strategic fallacy—was only window-dressing for the Russians. Their essential project is to create more ties with Europe, the planet's leading industrial power. Paying attention to the flow of imports and exports allows one to appreciate the real stakes of the subtle three-handed game that is preparing itself between Russia, the United States, and Europe.

In 2001 Russia and the United States did 10 billion euros of business with each other, Russia and the European Union did 7.5 times more or roughly 75 billion euros worth. Russia can get along without the United States but not without Europe. Russia is implicitly offering Europe a counterweight to American military influence and a secure supply of its energy requirements. It is a tempting offer.

No matter how intelligent Brzezinski's book was, the chessboard metaphor in his title was like a Freudian slip, a sort of unconscious intimation of the possibility of losing. Since it is their national sport, one ought to avoid playing chess with Russians. They are mentally well trained and will not make the mistake that their opponent is expecting—for example, reacting stupidly to provocations with no real strategic importance in Georgia and Uzbekistan. To refuse a piece offered by one's opponent, or an exchange of pieces, or a minor isolated conflict—these are the basics of chess. Especially when one is in a weak position. Maybe one day in diplomacy textbooks there will be an account of "The Putin Defense" that will explain how to achieve a reversal of alliances from a position of weakness and limited power.

However, we ought not overestimate the importance of calculation and conscious choice on the part of governments. The world's equilibrium does not depend fundamentally on the actions of Bush II and his court nor on the political intelligence of Putin. The dynamism or lack of dynamism of Russian society is the major factor worth watching. On this score it would seem Russia is in the process of emerging from a decade of chaotic fallout related to the end of communism and about to return to being a stable and trustworthy force within the balance of world power. However, it would be unwise to overidealize the present situation.

THE DEMOGRAPHIC PARAMETERS OF THE RUSSIAN CRISIS

Russian society is totally literate, and secondary and postsecondary education are quite advanced. But Russia remains poor and extremely violent. At the end of the 1990s Russian society was one of the rare cases in the world that combined a very high homicide rate, 23 for 100,000 inhabitants, and an equally high suicide rate, 35 for 100,000 inhabitants. These figures are each among the highest in the world.

Only Columbia surpasses the level of private violence in Russian society. Columbia has a level of anarchy that can only be described as madness even if part of this folly is articulated in the semicoherent, pseudorevolutionary language of the FARC (Revolutionary Armed Forces of Columbia). Suicide and homicide are the two main reasons behind the low life expectancy of Russian men. Already low in the last days of the Soviet Union, sixty-four years in 1989, the average length of life fell to a low of fifty-seven years in 1994. This average went up slightly, to sixty-one years in 1998, but was followed by a slight decrease, to sixty years, in 1999.

Changes in the rate of infant mortality allow one to follow the dramatic shocks of the postcommunist years. From 17.6 per 1000 in 1990, the infant mortality rate went as high as 20.3 in 1993. It went down again to 16.5 in 1998 before going back up slightly to 16.9 in 1999. The territorial heterogeneity across the Russian Federation makes it impossible to say that this latest upturn represents a significant change for mainstream Russia. The last two figures, while certainly not outstanding when compared to the rest of the developed world, are nevertheless the lowest figures in Russian history.

The most worrisome demographic data with obvious implications concerns the sharp drop in the birth rate. Best estimates place the birth rate in Russia for the year 2001 at 1.2. The same rate exists in Belarus and it is even lower, 1.1, in Ukraine. These figures do not necessarily imply an ongoing cultural practice specific to the Soviet territory since, being very low, they are almost indistinguishable from the situation in Central and Southern Europe. Spain's birth rate, we may recall, stands at 1.2, in Italy, Germany, and Greece it is 1.3. Given the high Russian death rates, the low birth rate will, according to the latest projections, lead to an important drop in population in the near future. From 144 million inhabitants in 2001, the Russian population will likely fall to 137 million by 2025. In Ukraine the population is expected to fall from 49 million to 45 million over the same period. These projections are of course based on the currently very unfavorable socioeconomic conditions. However the situation is changing and often improving.

ECONOMIC RECOVERY AND THE RETURN OF THE STATE

Since 1999 the Russian economy has started moving again. After a period of shrinking GNP (-4.8 percent in 1998), there has finally been a succession of positive growth—5.4 percent, 8.3 percent, and 5.5 percent for the years 1999–2001. This growth is not simply the result of oil and gas exports that have always been the strength of the Russian economy in good and bad years. Russian industry grew by an estimated 11–12 percent in 1999 and 2000. Particularly important sectors are mechanical construction, chemicals, petrochemicals, and paper. The recovery of light industry is also substantial. Russia seems to be surmounting its troubled past. It is no longer a country in sheer free fall as it once appeared to be. The process that led to the collapse of the currency in favor of a barter economy in some areas seems to have stopped, and there is renewed confidence in the currency's use. The state that seemed on the verge of evaporating has reemerged as an autonomous force in Russian social life—a phenomenon that can be measured in the most simple and fundamental terms by its renewed capacity to acquire a portion of the nation's wealth through tax collection and other means. As a proportion of GNP the resources of the state went from 8.9 percent in 1998 to 12.6 percent in 1999 and 16 percent in 2000. In 2000 there was a budget surplus that represented 2.3 percent of GNP.[1]

TABLE 10. Infant Mortality and Male Life Expectancy in Russia

1965	27.0	64.6
1966	25.6	64.3
1967	25.6	64.2
1968	25.5	63.9
1969	24.4	63.5
1970	22.9	63.2
1971	21.0	63.2
1972	21.6	63.2
1973	22.2	63.2
1974	22.6	63.2
1975	23.6	62.8
1976	24.8	62.3
1977	21.4	62.0
1978	23.5	61.8
1979	22.6	61.7
1980	22.0	61.5
1981	21.5	61.5
1982	20.2	62.0
1983	19.8	62.3
1984	21,2	62.0
1985	20.8	62.3
1986	19.1	63.8
1987	19.4	65.0
1988	19.1	63.8
1989	18.1	64.2
1990	17.6	63.8
1991	18.1	63.5
1992	20.3	58.9
1993	20.3	58.9
1994	18.6	57.3
1995	18.2	58.2
1996	17.5	59.7
1997	17.2	60.9
1998	16.5	61.3
1999	16.9	59.9

SOURCE: *Statistiques démographiques des pays industriels,* a database of France's Insitut National d'Études Démographiques (INED) developed by Alain Monnier and Catherine de Guibert-Lantoine.

The indispensable internal recovery of the equilibrium of Russian society and the reemergence of the state have two consequences on the international level. Russia can once again present itself as a reliable financial partner because it is seen to be servicing its foreign debt with no difficulty. Also, faced with the uncertain and aggressive behavior of the United States, Russia has been able to begin reestablishing a minimal military capacity — only 1.7 percent of GNP was devoted to defense spending in 1998, but this rose to 2.4 percent in 1999 and 2.7 percent in 2000. It would be no more than a wild guess to claim Russia has solved all its problems, or even the most important ones, but it is clear that the Putin era is one of stabilization for Russian social life and the beginning of the resolution of economic problems.

The rough-and-tumble attempt to open up the economy in the years 1990–1997 with the help of American advisors led the country into chaos. On this point we can accept Gilpin's account of how the breakdown of the state was largely responsible for the social and economic anarchy of Russia's transitional period.[2] China was able to avoid this kind of disaster by maintaining an authoritarian state apparatus at the center of the liberalizing process of the Chinese economy.

DEMOCRACY IN RUSSIA?

The question of economic dynamism is not the only uncertainty weighing on Russia's future. The other fundamental unknown is the fate of the political system, something no one can guarantee will be democratic and liberal. Western television and newspapers assure us every day that Vladimir Putin's Russia is undergoing a strict regimentation of its media. One after another television stations and newspapers are being forced to obey state authority, even if, as Western media admit, sometimes the goal is to break up oligarchies that were formed during the anarchic pseudoliberal years between 1990 and 2000, not to deny freedom of the press. One must remember that not that long ago in France, the state had monopolistic control over television that was eventually contested and broken up. But no reasonable person would have described the France of General de Gaulle as a country marching toward totalitarianism.

In Russia there is a president with strong powers elected by universal suffrage. There is also a parliament, less powerful, but also elected by universal suffrage. There are a number of different political parties that, like in France, are funded by the state instead of by large corporations as in America. There are three principal powers: a communist party, a centrist governmental power, and a free-market right. Like the Japanese, the Russian democracy has not taken the classic form of an alternating or rotating ruling party such as in France and in Anglo-Saxon countries. If this system proves stable, it would be an example of a democratic form adapted to a communitarian anthropological base.

Led by the centrist government, the Russian democracy is no doubt going through a phase of discipline after the anarchic decade of the 1990s. In Chechnya on the border of the federation, Putin's government is conducting a dirty war in ways that can legitimately be denounced. But given the innumerable ethnic minorities within the federation, it must be granted that preventing the Russian state from quelling Chechen opposition means consigning it to an eventual death by fragmentation. The activity of the CIA in the Caucasus over the last ten years and the deployment of military advisors in Georgia give the Chechen conflict an international dimension. It is a confrontation between Russia and America that is taking place there, and the two powers ought to divide fairly the moral responsibility for the human tragedy that has occurred.

If we want to judge Russia, we should adopt a broader perspective and refuse the historical myopia of day-to-day reports.

We ought to think comprehensively of all that Russia has been able to achieve in the midst of enormous social and economic suffering.

By itself Russia overthrew the most complete totalitarian regime in human history. It accepted without violent resistance the independence of its satellites in Eastern Europe, as well as the Baltic republics and those in the Caucasus and Central Asia. It accepted the breakup of the properly Russian center of the state with the splitting off of Belarus and Ukraine. It even allowed the independence movement of many territories to advance despite the presence of large ethnically Russian minorities. However nothing should be overidealized. One can point out that Russia often had no real choice in the matter and that leaving these minorities in place outside Russia allows for the possibility of exploiting their presence later. If that is true, one has to admire the wisdom and mastery of the Russian leaders who preferred gambling on a far-off future instead of succumbing immediately to an easy but useless violence. In a relatively short amount of time since the days when it enjoyed superpower status, Russia pacifically accepted all the defections and devolutions that Milosivic's Serbia refused. Achieving this, Russia proved itself to be a truly great nation, both calculating and responsible—a nation that, despite the horrors of Stalinism, we will be forced one day to admit has made a positive contribution to human history. This contribution includes one of the most universal of world literatures with Gogol, Tolstoy, Dostoyevsky, Chekhov, Turgenev, and many others. An account of Russian history cannot be limited to a retrospective denunciation of communism.

RUSSIAN UNIVERSALISM

In order to evaluate the benefits that Russia could offer the world now, we ought to first try and understand why the country had such a strong influence on the world in the past. Communism, a doctrine and practice of servitude invented by Russia, seduced a wide array of people outside the Soviet empire, from ordinary workers and peasants to professors, and in so doing transformed a local communist aspiration into a global force. Communism owed much of its success to the widespread existence, especially in central Eurasia, of egalitarian and authoritarian family structures that are predisposed to find communist ideology natural and acceptable. But Russia was for a time successful at organizing this ideology on a global scale and became the heart of an ideological empire. Why?

Russia's temperament is universalist. Equality was inscribed in the heart of the Russian peasant family structure by a rule of inheritance that was absolutely symmetrical. Under Peter the Great, the Russian nobles rejected primogeniture, the rule of inheritance that favors the eldest son to the detriment of the other siblings. Like the French peasants who had become literate before the French Revolution, the Russian peasants who became literate in the twentieth century spontaneously considered all men as a priori equal. Communism spread as a universalist doctrine offered to the world with, I admit, tragic and disappointing results. This universalist approach allowed for the transformation of the Russian empire into the Soviet Union. Bolshevism drew the empire's minorities into its circles of power—Baltics, Jews, Georgians, and Armenians. Like France, Russia's seductiveness flowed from its capacity to treat all men as equals.

Communism fell apart. The anthropological base of the former Soviet sphere is changing, slowly. The new Russian democracy, however, if it succeeds, will retain certain basic characteristics, and we should keep them in mind if we want to anticipate its likely future behavior on the international scene. A liberal Russian economy will never be an individualist Anglo-Saxon style capitalism. It will keep communitarian features, creating horizontal associative forms that it is too early to define more precisely. The political system is unlikely to function along the lines of the alternating two-party English and American model. Anyone who wants to speculate about the future shape of Russia ought to read the classic study by Anatole Leroy-Beaulieu, *L'Empire des tsars et les russes* (1897–1898).[3] It contains a comprehensive description of the behaviors and institutions marked by Russia's communitarian sensibility twenty to forty years *before* the triumph of communism.

A universalist approach to international politics will subsist with reflexes and instinctive reactions close to those of France such as, for example, the way France irritates the United States by its "egalitarian" approach to the Israeli-Palestinian question. Unlike Americans, Russians do not go around thinking there is an a priori borderline separating real men from everyone else—Indians, blacks, and Arabs. They have also not exterminated Indians at least since the conquest of Siberia in the seventeenth century. The survival of Bashkirs, Ostiaks, Maris, Samoyeds, Buryats, Tungus, Yakuts, Yukaghirs, and Chukchees testifies to the complex structure of the Russian Federation.

The Russian universalist temperament is cruelly lacking in international politics today. The dissolution of the Soviet Union, and with it a certain egalitarian angle on international relations, explains in part the unleashing of differentialist tendencies among Americans, Israelis, and others. The theme of France's little universalist music is faint indeed without the power of Russia as amplifier. The return of Russia within the international balance of power can only help the United Nations Organization. If Russia can avoid the pitfalls of anarchy and authoritarianism, it could become a fundamental balancing force in the world—a strong, nonhegemonic nation expressing an egalitarian understanding of the relations between peoples. This attitude will be all the easier to maintain since, unlike the United States, Russia does not rely on asymmetrical levies throughout the world for its raw materials, finished goods, capital, or oil.

STRATEGIC AUTONOMY

Given its persistent difficulties in the areas of population, safety, and public health, the recovery of Russia cannot be counted on at present as a definitive element within the new global order. But we should nevertheless go as far as we can with this hypothesis and examine the specific benefits of a Russian economy that has regained its balance and possibilities for growth. We can make one immediate observation: Russia would be a unique economic power, combining a relatively high level of training among its active population and total energy independence. A comparison with Great Britain, which has oil reserves in the North Sea, would be superficial. The oil- and especially gas-producing capacity of Russia makes the country a major player when it comes to the world's energy future. One must also keep in mind the immense quantity of other natural resources that lie within its very large territory. In contrast to the dependent United States, nature has granted Russia a high level of independence from the rest of the world. Russia also has a positive trade balance.

This situation owes nothing to human choice, but it does have an effect on the definition of social systems. The territorial mass of Russia and its wealth in minerals and energy made the Stalinist conception of "socialism in one country" possible. Amidst the debate over globalization and interdependence, Russia could emerge—if everything works out for the best—as an enormous democracy with a balanced trade budget and energy autonomy. In a world dominated by the United States, it would be the incarnation of De Gaulle's dream of independence.

If part of the weakness in Washington comes from uncertainty as to how America will guarantee its necessary supply of money and merchandise, especially oil, over the near term, we can note the symmetrical contrast among Russian leaders who can afford to be calm and collected. If they can stabilize their institutions and borders, in Chechnya or elsewhere, they know they will be beholden to no one. They already have a rare advantage—the ability to export oil and, more important, natural gas. The structural weakness of Russia is demographic, but this weakness, we will see, could work out in its favor. Ironically, all this makes post-communist Russia a mostly reassuring nation, since it is not dependent for its energy on the rest of the world, unlike the United States whose new predator status is worrisome.

RECENTERING THE RUSSIAS

The number one priority for Russia, however, is not its image abroad but, rather, the task of rebuilding the idea of its own strategic sphere, something neither exactly foreign nor domestic. The former Soviet Union had a very particular structure partly inherited from the Czarist era, and for this reason perhaps slightly more permanent than the breakup of the communist period would suggest. Russia is composed of two rings: first, a Slavic core of Russians in a broad sense. This is traditionally designated by the expression "All the Russias" and includes, besides the central entity, Belarus and Ukraine. The second ring is composed of all the other entities of the Community of Independent States in the Caucasus and Central Asia. The recovery of the Russian economy could little by little revive this whole ensemble and recreate the former Russian sphere of influence without any domination in the traditional sense.

This process, if it moves forward, will owe as much to the inability of Western economies, badly weakened by the slowdown of capitalism, to occupy the vacuum that has existed for the last decade as it will to the rekindling of the economy in the Russian center of these two rings. Only the three Baltic republics are really engaged in the European or, more precisely, Scandinavian sphere. The reemergence of the "Soviet" sphere is no more certain than the definitive recovery of Russia, but one can already see that the recovery need not be spectacular for this recentering of the Russias to take place. There exist anthropological affinities among all the nations built out of the ruins of the USSR that go back much further than the communist era.

All the countries of the sphere, without exception, had communitarian family structures that associated in the traditional society a father and his married sons. This is true of the Baltic region, the Caucasus, and Central Asia. The only observable difference is the endogamic preference, sometimes minimal, of certain Islamized populations such as the Azerbaijanis, Uzbeks, Kirghiz, Tajiks, and Turkmens. The Kazaks, on the other hand, are exogamic like the Russians. This anthropological link can in no way lead to the extinction of these peoples. The Latvians, Estonians, Georgians, and Armenians still exist as much as the Muslim peoples, even if the nations born from the decomposition of communism sometimes owe a lot in Central Asia to a political "fabrication" borrowed from Sovietism, as Olivier Roy has observed.[4] But one must remember that real cultural affinities still exist among the peoples of the former Soviet Union, in particular an omnipresent communitarian sensibility. The progress of democracy throughout this zone is happening, but there is a fundamental resistance to all expressions of overly violent individualism. This common anthropological base allows us to explain a recent phenomenon here and now, as well as to predict a future one concerning the development of postcommunist society over the whole territory of the former USSR.

The recent phenomenon: the revolution toward liberalism started in Russia, the leading center of the system, and has not spread that fast to the periphery republics where individualism is no more natural than in Russia. The independence of these outer republics, Slavic or non-Slavic, shielded them from this liberal Russian revolution and has encouraged the fossilization of regimes more authoritarian than in Russia.

The future phenomenon: the future of democracy among the entities in the outermost ring of the Russian system will be influenced to a great extent by the weight of Russia—at least as much if not more than by a weak or inappropriately adapted Western influence. Russia is in the process of looking for and defining the path to an exit out of communism—this means the definition of a liberalized economic and political regime but one capable of taking into account its strong communitarian sensibility. In this restrained sense it could again become a model for the whole region.

The existence of a common anthropological base among all the republics of the former Soviet Union explains why it is possible to identify similar cultural traits throughout this zone—for example, in the area of violence, both homicide and suicide. The only countries with a violence-related death rate as spectacular as Russia are Ukraine, Belarus, Kazakstan, and the three Baltic republics—Estonia, Latvia, and Lithuania. The parallel is so strong that it could not be completely explained by the presence of Russian minorities, even large ones as in Estonia and Latvia. At the level of state organization and political thinking within states the Soviet sphere has yet to really disappear.

At the moment of their independence the Baltic republics rushed to invent a history of eternal opposition to Russia, something that is not very believable from the standpoint of anthropological analysis. North and Central Russia, the birthplace of the Russian state, and the Baltic republics belong to a common cultural zone, strongly communitarian in family structures and in its ideological aspirations during the transition toward modernity. A map of the Bolshevik voters in the founding election of the Assembly in 1917 shows that communist support was stronger in Latvia than in Northern and Central Russia. The contribution of Latvians to the Soviet secret police was significant from the start. Therefore, it is not surprising to observe among psychological indicators such as rates of homicide and suicide a persistent overlap between Russian and Baltic cultures.

On the other hand, the very low suicide rate in Azerbaijan is typical of a Muslim country because Islam with its typically close-knit and warm family structure seems always to confer an immunity to self-destruction. But the suicide rates in the other Muslim republics of Central Asia are too high for Muslim countries, and the same is true for Kazakstan where half the population is Russian. This deviation suggests a stronger Soviet influence than is generally admitted. To this fact can be added the complete literacy, the low birth rates, and the insignificance of Islamism in post-Soviet Central Asia. In his remarkable studies, Olivier Roy perhaps underestimates the impact of Russian culture in the region. He hardly sees any trace besides the Russian language, the lingua franca of the ruling classes in Central Asia, a phenomenon he imagines to be temporary.[5] While I would not believe for a minute the idea of an underground survival of the Soviet sphere, I would proceed more carefully if I were an American geo-strategist. The fifteen thousand U.S. soldiers Washington has stationed in Uzbekistan are far from home in more ways than one and hardly significant in numbers. A strike force today, they could find themselves hostages tomorrow.

THE UKRAINIAN QUESTION

Between 1990 and 1998 the breakdown of the Russian order went very far, leading ultimately to the Russian state's loss of control over ethnically Russian populations. In the case of the Baltic states and in the Caucasus and Central Asia, the loss of control can be interpreted as imperial retreat or decolonization. However, in the case of Belarus, Ukraine, and the northern half of Kazakstan, Russia lost a part of its traditional sphere of domination. Belarus had never existed before as an autonomous state. Neither had the north of Kazakstan, and in these two cases the loss of control may be considered as the surprising effect of an anarchy that nevertheless chose to respect the borders created during the Soviet era. Ukraine, with its three subpopulations— Uniate Ukrainians in the west, Orthodox Ukrainians in the center, and Russians in the east—is a more complex case. A more realistic definitive secession could have been imagined. Nevertheless, Huntington is probably closer to the truth than Brzezinski when he says that Ukraine is likely to be pulled back within the Russian orbit. However, one need not accept his simplistic religious interpretation of the situation. Ukraine's dependency on Russia is the result of more dense, subtle, and longstanding historical ties.

For Ukraine, innovation has always come from Russia. This has been a historical constant. The Bolshevik revolution was born in Russia, and more precisely in its historically dominant part—the vast area around the Moscow-St. Petersburg axis. The Russian state was born there, and from there emanated every wave of modernization from the sixteenth to the twentieth century. And it is there that the liberalizing movement began in the 1990s. The fall of communism and the wave of reforms being pursued today started in Moscow and are being carried out via the Russian language. Cut off from Russia, Ukraine will only be able to pursue reforms at a very slow pace, the ideological agitation and lobbying of the International Monetary Fund notwithstanding.

Historically and sociologically Ukraine is no more than a vague, badly structured area that has never been the origin of any important events of modernization. It is essentially a Russian tributary, subject to the shocks from the center and at all times characterized by its conservatism—anti-Bolshevik and anti-Semitic in 1917–1918 and more attached to Stalinism than Russia in 1990. Westerners, deceived by its western geographic position and by the presence of a large religious minority of Uniates who are close to Catholicism, have not understood that Ukrainian independence was a move to isolate itself from the Moscow-St. Petersburg-inspired democratic revolution, even if it had the side effect of

TABLE 11. Rates of Homicide and Suicide in the World
(per 100,000 Inhabitants)

	Homicide	Suicide	Total
Russia 1998	22.9	35.3	58.2
Belarus 1999	11.1	33.5	44.6
Ukraine 1999	12.5	28.8	41.3
Estonia 1999	16.1	33.2	49.3
Latvia 1999	12.7	31.4	44.1
Lithuania 1999	8.0	42.0	50.0
Azerbaijan 1999	4.7	0.7	5.4
Kazakstan 1999	16.4	26.8	43.2
Kyrgyzstan 1999	7.0	11.5	18.5
Uzbekistan 1999	6.8	3.3	10.1
Tajikistan 1995	6.1	3.4	9.5
Turkmenistan 1998	8.4	6.9	15.3
Germany 1998	0.9	14.2	15.1
United States 1998	6.6	11.3	17.9
Finland 1998	2.4	23.8	26.2
France 1997	0.9	19.9	19.9
Hungary 1999	2.9	33.1	36.0
Japan 1997	0.6	18.6	19.2
United Kingdom 1998	0.7	7.4	8.1
Sweden 1996	1.2	14.2	15.4
Argentina 1994	4.6	6.4	11.0
Columbia 1994	73.0	3.2	20.4
Mexico 1995	17.2	3.2	20.4
Venezuela 1994	15.7	5.1	20.8

SOURCE: *Demographic Yearbook of the United Nations*

obtaining for itself Western investment. However, we ought not exaggerate Ukraine's peripheral conservatism. The difficulties it has had trying to pull out of pure presidential authoritarianism are not comparable to those encountered in Kazakstan or Uzbekistan.

The scenario proposed by Brzezinski was not absurd. Ukraine has enough cultural differences with Russia to allow it to take on its own identity. But without a social dynamic of its own Ukraine can only escape Russian control by being pulled into the orbit of another power. The force of America is too far away and too immaterial to serve as a counterweight to Russia. Europe is a real economic force with Germany at its center, but it is not a military or political force. But if Europe wants to acquire these latter dimensions, it is not in its interest to grasp at Ukraine because it will need Russia as a counterbalance to emancipate itself from American control.

Here we can take the measure of America's concrete economic nonexistence in the heart of Central Asia. Words alone cannot compensate for its lack of industrial production, especially for a developing country such as Ukraine. Besides some weaponry and a few computers, America does not have a lot to offer. It does not export the industrial and consumer goods the Ukrainians need. As for investment capital, the United States hogs most of it for itself, thus depriving the developing world of financial resources generated by the economies of Europe and Japan. All that America can do is hold up the illusion of being a financial power by maintaining political and ideological control over the IMF and the World Bank—two institutions, we may note in passing, Russia can now do without, thanks to its trade surplus.

America can of course treat itself to the goods that will eventually be produced in Ukraine and pay for this consumption with money that it has siphoned from Europe, Japan, or elsewhere. But a look at Ukraine's business transactions reveals both its dependence on Russia and Europe and the outsider status of the United States. In 2000 Ukraine imported a little more than 2 billion dollars worth of goods from the Community of Independent States and almost 5 billion dollars worth from the rest of the world, principally Europe.[6] The 190 million dollars in goods and services from theUnited States represented only 1.4 percent of the total.[7] In the same year Ukraine exported nearly 4.5 billion dollars worth of goods and services to the CIS and 10 billion to the rest of the world, including 872 million to the U.S., or 6 percent of the total. Ukraine covers only 56 percent of its expenditures on imports from CIS with its revenues from exports, but with the rest of the world it has a trade surplus of 170 percent.

This is where the immateriality of the American empire shows up most clearly—the United States only covers 22 percent of its imports with Ukraine with its revenues from exports back to that country. We can also note the evolution of this process over time. The United States has had a trade deficit with Ukraine only since 1994. In 1992 and 1993 it enjoyed a small trade surplus. It is more and more clear that consuming is the fundamental specialty of the American economy within the international system. The United States is very far away from the situation of overproduction that it experienced immediately after the Second World War. That is why it was not able to propose a second Marshall Plan, which the countries coming out of communism really needed. In the former Soviet sphere, as elsewhere, the United States is no longer the giver but the taker.

The only thing we can be sure of about Ukraine is that it is not going to move. Close ties with Russia are as probable as its pure and simple seizure by Moscow seems impossible. If its economy reignites, Russia will become the center of gravity of an area beyond its own borders. The Community of Independent States could become a real and novel political formation, combining Russian leadership and the autonomy of a succession of outer rings. Belarus would be for all practical purposes annexed, Ukraine would remain autonomous but as a second Little- or New-Russia. The notion of "All the Russias" would reemerge within the local and international consciousness. Beyond the Caucasus, Armenia would remain an ally bound to Russia by its fear of Turkey, the privileged ally for a few more years of the United States. Georgia would rejoin the fold. The Central Asian republics would return explicitly to Russian influence, with the half-Russian Kazakstan playing of course a particularly important role in the region. The reemergence of Russia as a dynamic economic and cultural actor in this region would necessarily put the troops stationed by the United States in Uzbekistan and Kyrgyztan in a strange situation—truly "foreign bodies" in every sense of the term. This process of reorganization would create directly to the east of Europe a second plurinational entity with, in its case, a single central directing force, Russia. But with both of these large entities the complexity of the political system would make all truly aggressive behavior difficult and any entry into a major military conflict extremely problematic.

WEAKNESS AS STRENGTH

My portrait of Russia, ideal and necessary to the world's health, is perhaps a bit prettier than is warranted. I have described a virtual nation. For the moment, as we have noted, there is more violence in Russia than almost anywhere else in the world. The state is struggling to maintain its ability to collect taxes and preserve the integrity of its borders in the Caucasus. It has to put up with the performance-oriented more than truly performative circling by the Americans in Georgia and Uzbekistan. The Western press strikes a pose of perverse angelic naïveté to reproach Russians for their regulated media, their far right youth groups, and all other imperfections of a country waking up from great pain. Many Western media that have grown soft after years of overdevelopment are giving all of us a frisson with their portrait of a raw, edgy Russia.

As for the American strategists, their approach is to endlessly explain that for the long-term security of the West we have to make sure the Russians understand that their empire days are over. In doing so they are no doubt hinting at their concern over the longevity of the American empire. No sophisticated intellectual speculation is necessary to understand that Russia is no longer an expanding force. No matter what form its regime takes, democratic or authoritarian, Russia is shrinking demographically. Its population is decreasing and aging, and this factor alone permits us to view the nation as a stabilizing force rather than a threat.

From an American standpoint this demographic movement has produced something rather surprising. At first the contraction of the Russian population, added to the collapse of their economy, made the United States the only remaining superpower and started Washington dreaming about an impossible empire. At that time there arose the temptation to kill the Russian bear for good. Lately, however, the world is realizing little by little that a diminished Russia is not a source of worry but on the contrary is becoming almost automatically a balancing force in a situation made disturbing by an America that has become too powerful, too predatory, and too erratic in its international actions. This is what allowed Vladimir Putin to make the following declaration in Berlin: "No one doubts the great value of European relations with the United States. But I think that Europe would consolidate its reputation as a truly independent global force . . . if it associated its capacities with those of Russia—with its human, territorial, and natural resources and the economic, cultural, and defense potential of Russia."

When it comes right down to it, we are not absolutely sure that Russia is going to establish a democratic society and prove forever, or at least for a long time, Fukuyama's dream-hypothesis about the universalization of the liberal society. In this political area Russia is not fully reliable. But it is reliable in the area of diplomacy for two essential reasons. First, because Russia is weak. Paradoxically, along with the internal stabilization of the country, weakness is Vladimir Putin's major advantage, one that is allowing him to reinsert Russia as a potential ally on the European chessboard. But Russia is also reliable because, liberal or not, it has a universalist temperament capable of perceiving international relations in a just, egalitarian way. When linked to its weakness that prevents delusions of grand domination, Russian universalism can only be a positive contribution to the equilibrium of the world.

This very optimistic vision of Russia as a balancing force would not even be necessary for a "realist" of the classic American school, whether of the Kissinger type or another. For a strategic realist the military counterweight does not need to be morally good. >

The Greeks, finally tired of Athenian power, eventually called on Sparta for help. Sparta was not a model of democracy and liberty but had the unique advantage of refusing all territorial expansion. Thus ended the Athenian empire, done in by Greeks not Persians. It would be ironic in the years ahead to see Russia play the role of Sparta, an oligarchical city called on to defend liberty, after having long played the role of Persia, a multiethnic empire threatening all nations. No comparison ought to be pushed too far. The world of today is too vast and complex to permit a new Peloponnesian War—quite simply because America does not have the economic, military, or ideological resources to keep its European and Japanese allies from reasserting their liberty if they so desire.

8

The Emancipation of Europe

For Europeans, the weeks following the attacks of September 11 were an occasion for a wonderful demonstration of solidarity. Their leaders promised to strongly involve NATO—a defensive alliance above the power of single states—in a positive if poorly defined "war on terrorism." However, over the next twelve months relations between America and Europe steadily deteriorated. The real reasons for this were as seemingly mysterious as its development seemed inexorable. The violence of the terrorist attacks was the catalyst of the early solidarity. The American war on terrorism, brutal and inefficient in its methods and obscure as to its real objectives, ended up fueling a true antagonism between Europe and America. The relentless denunciation of an "axis of evil," the constant support of Israel, and the contempt for Palestinians all progressively changed the view Europeans had of the United States. Formerly perceived as a peacemaker, America had become a troublemaker. Europeans who had for long been loyal children of a respected paternal power began to suspect this supreme authority of a possibly dangerous lack of responsibility. And though far from complete, there began to emerge the unthinkable—a common international sensibility uniting the French, German, and British peoples.

Coming from the French, suspicion of the United States is nothing new. The change among the Germans, on the other hand, is stupefying. The obedience of the leaders of the principal Western protectorate, an indispensable means for exerting American influence over the continent, was a given back in Washington. This implicit pact was anchored by two unpronounceable truths. First, the United States crushed Germany with its bombings from 1943 to 1945, and second, Germans are by nature an obedient people who submit to the stronger force. They are also grateful to America for protecting Germany from communism and for allowing their economic development. The loyalty of Germany seemed sealed for eternity by a combination of mutually understood relations of force and shared interests.

The new hesitancy on the part of America's British ally is no less surprising. The alignment of Great Britain alongside the United States was a fact of nature for American strategic analysts—a congenital condition solidly affirmed in a shared language, temperament, and civilization. The unthinking casualness with which Brzezinski speaks of British support is typical. The emergence of a new English anti-Americanism—on the left and the right—may seem surprising since it is erupting in the wake of an unprecedented collaboration with the Americans in Afghanistan. After all, Britain did manage to stay out of the Vietnam War. But the phenomenon of a return to distance after a period of intense proximity is a classic scenario that all the countries of Europe have experienced in one way or another. After getting too close to something or someone, one may become aware of intolerable differences.

A detailed analysis of the press of each country in the "Old Europe" that belongs to NATO would show the rise in fear and then exasperation. It is simpler, however, to note the effects of these changed feelings. Despite the furious opposition of American military and civilian leaders, Europeans have managed to agree on the construction of an Airbus for military transport. They have also initiated the satellite tracking system Galileo in order to break up the monopoly of the American GPS system. This decision demonstrated the substantial economic and technological force of Europe, since the project requires the placement of some thirty satellites in orbit. Where there's a will—that is, when the Germans, British, and French are in agreement—there is a European way. In June 2002, with Great Britain and Germany in agreement, Europe showed itself capable of threatening the United States with countermeasures in response to the latter's increase of steel import tariffs. International conferences are now full of American leaders—from academia, the military, and the media—who are often extremely bitter about Europeans' lack of understanding and loyalty while silently blaming them for being wealthy, powerful, and increasingly autonomous.

This evolution can only be superficially explained by the events of a single year or two. Media-soaked episodes of recent political discord have served as the means for a certain consciousness-raising but do not get at the real substance of the antagonism. Profound forces are at work. Some are bringing Europeans and Americans closer together, others are pushing them apart. A proper analysis is made more difficult by one important aspect of the current process: the centrifugal and centripetal forces are increasing simultaneously. In Europe a growing desire to fuse with the United States is being increasingly and more strongly countered by the opposing wish to dissociate itself from the United States. Among couples this kind of tension is typical of the stage that precedes divorce.

THE TWO OPTIONS: IMPERIAL INTEGRATION
OR INDEPENDENCE?

Since World War II, the relation of European leaders to the United States has been as ambivalent as the relation of Washington's leaders toward the construction of Europe. America needed a Franco-German reconciliation in order to assure the coherence of NATO on the continent in the face-off with Russia, but it never imagined a reconciliation that would lead to the birth of a competing strategic entity. The progressive slide from sympathy and encouragement to suspicion then bitterness and finally opposition is understandable.

As for European leaders, they very reasonably appreciated the need for American protection following the Prague coup in 1948 and other Soviet encroachments in Eastern Europe. Now that the hangover from the Second World War is gone, and communism too, they are naturally overtaken by a combination of doubts and nostalgia about independence. After all, from the point of view of the ruling classes in the countries of "Old Europe," each of their national histories is longer, richer, and more interesting than that of the United States, which reaches back only three centuries. Having caught up with the American standard of living, it was inevitable that Europeans would begin to doubt the legitimacy of American leadership and start thinking seriously about their emancipation. For the same reasons, the same applies to Japan on the other side of Eurasia.

But opposing forces pushing in the direction of a total integration within the American system also appeared in the last twenty years. The liberal economic revolution (or ultraliberal reaction, in the terminology of the left) produced at the highest European levels a new temptation. The developed world, as we have noted is being transformed by a rise in oligarchical tendencies. These newly emerging social forces are in need of a leader. At the very moment when their military role no longer seems necessary, the United States has become the global champion of a revolution in inequality and a mutation toward oligarchy that one can easily imagine is seductive to the ruling class within every society in the world. What America proposes now is not the protection of a liberal democracy, but instead more money and power for those who are already the wealthiest and the most powerful.

The European leaders from 1965 to 2000 did not definitively choose between the two options, integration or emancipation. They simultaneously liberalized the economy and unified the continent, thus placing the Americans in a novel position at the beginning of the twenty-first century—that of not being sure if their dependents were traitors or loyal subjects. Europe has become, as America wanted, a free-trade zone without tariffs, if, that is, one sets aside the remains of the Common Agricultural Policy. But the euro exists and its fall in value by 25 percent against the dollar between its creation and February 2002 did for a time reestablish a de facto protection of the European economy with regard to the United States by lowering the price of all European exports and raising the price of imports from America by the same percentage. The outcry from leaders and the media in "Old Europe" when the Bush administration reinstated protective tariffs on foreign steel and agricultural subsidies suggests that European leaders are not fully conscious of their actions. They do not want to recognize that the euro alone is already acting against the United States—first by its initial drop against the dollar and then by its later rise—because they have not yet really made their choice between integration within the American system and emancipation.

From the point of view of European leaders, the "imperial integration" option would require a double mental revolution—it would mean the burial of the nation-state and an imperial marriage. It would involve renouncing the defense of the independence of their peoples in exchange for which the happy few would be integrated as full-fledged members of the American ruling class. This was what was in the minds of a large cross-section of the French and other European elites on September 11 when everyone supposedly was feeling "*américain*." It was the generalized spread of the Jean-Marie Messier fantasy.[1]

The increasingly frequent and refined muggings of Europeans by Wall Street as well as American banks and corporations make the integration option less and less attractive. And now with the emergence on the American right of a veritable Euro-phobia one has to wonder if the country is not simply going to resolve the question itself by proving to its allies that there is no way they will ever be anything but second-class citizens in the eyes of America. The rise of American differentialism does not simply operate to the detriment of blacks, Hispanics, and Arabs. To a lesser degree it also concerns Europeans and the Japanese.

The "emancipation" option would result from the objective economic power of Europe and the recognition of shared values distinct from those of the United States. It would suppose a Europe capable of insuring its own military defense. On these criteria this option is realistically attainable in the very near future. Europe is industrially more powerful than the United States. It no longer has to fear Russia's seriously weakened military. It ought, however, seek to obtain true strategic autonomy by augmenting its nuclear strike force. This is a taboo subject, but the mutual fear that still exists between the United States and Russia leaves Europe plenty of time to build up this potential if it wants to. The only serious problem facing Europe is the low overall birth rate. This demographic deficit does not weaken it in relation to Russia, which has the same problem, but in relation to the United States.

Presenting these options suggests the possibility of making a choice. It is to imagine the ruling classes transformed into conscious actors, anthropomorphized, and deciding on a direction to take after weighing their interests, tastes, and values. Such marvelous feats no doubt have existed in the past. One thinks of the senate of the Roman republic, the leaders of the Athenian democracy at the time of Pericles, the Convention in France in 1793, the Victorian imperial elite at the time of Gladstone and Disraeli, and the Prussian aristocracy under Bismarck. We are not living in one of those grand times. At most one might claim there is a consciousness of this type among the current upper classes in America, but with certain reservations, since the option chosen, when there is a choice, is always the path of least resistance, a path that one may doubt has really been chosen at all. But in the case of the European ruling classes—those that still have some capacity to make difficult binding decisions—there is nothing but the illusion of thinking collectively because of the fragmentation of conflicting national agendas.

It is large-scale unconscious factors that are going to decide things when it comes to relations between Europe and America. The very nature of things, as one used to say, is going to force a separation between the two.

THE CONFLICT BETWEEN EUROPEAN AND AMERICAN CIVILIZATIONS

The forces of dissociation, however, are not only economic. Culture plays its role, even though the cultural dimension is impossible to distinguish completely from economics. The dominant values in Europe—rather foreign these days to American society—are agnosticism, peace, and balance.

Herein lies perhaps the greatest error of Huntington—his wish to restrain the sphere of American domination to what he calls the West. In seeking to put "civilized" clothes on American aggressiveness, he first sets up the Muslim world, Confucian China, and Orthodox Russia and against these postulates the existence of a "Western sphere" whose nature is quite uncertain even according to his own criteria. This patchwork West of his pieces together Catholics and Protestants in one and the same religious and cultural system. This fusion is shocking for anyone who has worked on the opposing differences between theologies and rituals, or more simply on the bloody battles between the faithful of these two religions in the sixteenth and seventeenth centuries.

Putting aside Huntington's inconsistent application of his own variable, religion, it is almost too easy to show the latent opposition between Europe and America when the criterion of religion is used correctly to analyze the present situation. America is swamped with religious discourses of all kinds, half of its citizens say they go to some weekend service, and a quarter in fact do go. Europe, on the other hand, is an agnostic space where religious services are practiced by an ever smaller number of people. However, the European Union does a better job than America at following the biblical commandment, "Thou shalt not kill." Capital punishment has been abolished, and the homicide rate is very low, only slightly more than 1 per 100,000 inhabitants. Executions in America are a routine affair and the homicide rate, even after a slight decrease, remains between 6 and 7 per 100,000 inhabitants. Here, America fascinates because it is different, not universal. In movies its violence seems interesting, but it is unbearable when it is exported in the form of diplomatic and military action. The number and variety of cultural differences between Europeans and Americans is almost infinite. Among these an anthropologist would have to mention the status of the American woman—a castrating, threatening figure almost as disturbing for European males as the all-powerful Arab man is for European females.

Above all, one must speak of the deepest and oldest divergence of the American and European worldviews that derives from the very means by which their respective societies were formed, a level of analysis where it is hardly possible to distinguish customs from economy and thus it is best to speak of different "civilizations."

European societies evolved from the labor of generations of miserable peasants. For centuries they suffered at the hands of warring ruling classes. They experienced wealth and peace only belatedly. One can say the same for Japan and for the large majority of the Old World. All of these societies maintain as part of their genetic code, as it were, an instinctive comprehension of the notion of economic equilibrium. On the level of moral practice one associates it with the notions of work and compensation, on the level of accounting with the notions of production and consumption.

American society, on the other hand, is the recent outcome of a highly successful colonial experience but one not tested by time—it developed over three centuries, thanks to the importation of literate workers to a world rich in minerals and other natural resources, and agriculturally productive, thanks to its virgin soil. America seems not to have understood that its success stems from a process of one-sided exploitation and expenditure of wealth that it did not create.

The strong understanding that Europeans, the Japanese, or any other people of Eurasia have about the necessity of an ecological balance and of a commercial balance is the outcome of a long peasant history. Since medieval times Europeans, Japanese, Chinese, and Indians, for example, have had to struggle against the impoverishment of their soils and face up to the scarcity of natural resources. In the United States a people supposedly liberated from the weight of the past discovered a seemingly inexhaustible natural abundance. In this context economics ceased to be the discipline for the study of the optimal allocation of scarce resources and became a religion of dynamic energy uninterested in the notion of equilibrium. America's refusal of the Kyoto ecology accord and its acceptance of the O'Neill doctrine concerning the benign character of trade imbalances are in part the consistent extension of its cultural traditions. America has always grown by playing out its soils, wasting its oil, and by looking abroad for the people it needed to do its work.

THE AMERICAN SOCIAL MODEL THREATENS EUROPE

In European societies people generally stay put. The mobility of European populations occurs at rates that are half of what they are throughout the United States—this includes England where the percentage of inhabitants changing residences in one year (1981) was only 9.6 percent, comparable to France's 9.4 percent and Japan's 9.5 percent as against 17.5 percent in the United States.[2] The residential instability of the American people is often cited as evidence of its dynamism; however, the current lag in production of American industry would seem to cast doubt on the intrinsic economic efficiency of this constant movement. After all, the Japanese produce twice as much while moving about half as much as the Americans.

In Europe the relation of citizens to the state was one of confidence, and remains so even on the subideological level of everyday thinking. The various institutions that constitute the state's very being are never viewed as enemies, whereas in the United States liberal ideology is only the most visible and publicly acceptable variant of an attitude toward the state that in the minds of many can run to extreme lengths of paranoia. In Germany, Italy, and even in Great Britain where the liberal revolution was much greater than in France, one does not find anything comparable to the armed militias in the United States whose declared mission is to resist the alleged manipulation emanating from the central state—or "federal government," to use the American terminology.[3] Social security is the keystone of every European society. This is why the United States' export of its specific model of unregulated capitalism constitutes a danger for European societies, as well as for Japan, a country that is close to its distant European cousins when it comes to these factors of social equilibrium.

During the last decade of the twentieth century there was much speculation about the varieties of capitalism—about the existence in Germany, for example, of an industrial Rhineland model that privileged social cohesiveness, stability, worker training, and long-term technological investment in contrast with a liberal Anglo-Saxon model that encouraged profits and the mobility of labor and capital over the short term. With some minor differences Japan would be close to the German economic model just as it is to the German anthropological base, the stem-family tradition most admired by Frédéric Le Play.[4] The strengths and weaknesses of each model were debated, with most commentators granting the superiority of the German or Japanese model in the 1980s and in the following decade an apparent rise in power, more ideological than industrial, of the Anglo-Saxon model.

The question of economic advantages and deficiencies is in a way becoming secondary. The American system is no longer able to provide for its own population. More seriously from a European perspective, the constant attempts to foist the liberal model onto the strongly rooted and state-centered societies of the Old World is in the process of blowing them apart—a phenomenon that can be observed nowadays in the regular gains of the far right in a number of recent elections. Denmark, the Netherlands, Belgium, France, Switzerland, Italy, and Austria have all been affected. A black circle seems to surround Germany that has acquired the rather surprising status, if one thinks of the 1930s, of being Europe's anti-fascist pole. England has not been affected, a fact that may be attributed to its greater ease when it comes to adapting to the ultraliberal model. But the country has grown nervous and is rediscovering a passion for government intervention on economic and social issues whether in education, public health, or the management of the railroads. Spain and Portugal know that their temporary immunity to the progress of the far right is only due to the relative belatedness of their economic development and the historical proximity of the fascist regimes of Franco and Salazar.

For the moment Germany and Japan have resisted. It is not that the two countries are more flexible or resilient in the face of social insecurity so much as it is a consequence of the fact that until recently these two super powerful economies protected the mass of workers and ordinary citizens. We can be certain that American-style deregulation within these socially cohesive nations will trigger a rise of the far right.

Here precisely the ideological and strategic balance falters. The type of capitalism that identifies with the American model is becoming a threat to the societies that had most successfully resisted it. After having benefited for a short time from free trade, the major industrial powers, Japan and Germany, are now choking from the insufficiency of world demand. Unemployment rates have risen even in Japan. The working classes can no longer be protected from the pressures of globalization. The ideological dominance of ultraliberalism led to the emergence within these societies of a discourse that in large and small ways is destructive of mental and political balance.

The American business press never tires of calling for the reform of these "unmodern" and "closed" systems whose only real crime is that they are too productive. In times of global depression the strongest industrial economies always suffer more than underdeveloped or underproductive societies. The crisis of 1929 struck at the heart of the United States' economy because of its industrial strength at the time. The sluggishly productive United States of the year 2000 is better equipped for confronting a drop in demand. Articles in the American business press that call for the modernization of the German and Japanese systems all have an unintended darkly comic side, since one might seriously wonder how the world economy could function if Germany and Japan began running up trade deficits on the scale of the United States. All the same the ideological pressure exerted by the United States, especially the dominance of liberal notions when it comes to the organization of trade on a worldwide scale, is becoming a fundamental problem for the two most important allies of the United States that also happen to be the two highest exporting industrial economies. At first the stability of the American system relied on Washington's domination of these two fundamental pillars, Germany and Japan, both conquered during the Second World War and then tamed. Led astray by its new intolerance for the rest of the world, America is in the process of alienating both of them.

In Europe the new behavior of Germany, the dominant economic power, is the important event. The liberal American revolution is much more threatening to German social cohesiveness than to the French republican model that combines individualism and state guarantees. In terms of social values the conflict between the United States and France is partial while the opposition between the German and American social conceptions is absolute. George W. Bush's trip through Europe in May of 2002 reflected this discrepancy between France and Germany. The anti-Bush demonstrations drew much larger crowds in Germany than in France. Until very recently the French, long under the charm of General de Gaulle, thought themselves the only one capable of independence. They have trouble conceiving of a Germany rebelling in the name of its own cherished values, and yet the emancipation of Europe, if it takes place, will owe as much to this German movement as to any French action.

Europeans are very conscious of the problems posed by the United States whose mass has been at the same time protective and oppressive for many years. They are much less conscious of the problems that they pose for the United States. Europe is often teased as the economic giant with no consciousness or capacity for political action. This criticism, very often justified, tends to forget, however, that economic strength is a force in itself and that the mechanisms of integration and concentration that result from it spontaneously produce strategic effects with both short- and long-term repercussions. This is why America felt threatened, even before the creation of the euro, by Europe's rise in economic power.

EUROPE'S ECONOMIC POWER

In practice, free trade does not produce a unified world even if it does stimulate the circulation of goods between continents. Globalization is only a secondary dimension of the process. The statistical reality shows instead the intensification of priority trading between geographically close neighbors and the establishment of integrated regional trading blocks of continental size: Europe, North and Central America, South America, the Far East. The rules of the liberal game set up by American leadership tend to undermine the hegemony of the United States by favoring the establishment of regional blocks separate from North America.

Europe is thus becoming an autonomous power almost in spite of itself. What is worse, from an American perspective, is that Europe stands to annex new spaces on its margins by virtue of their mere contiguity and existence as priority trading partners. Again, its force is expressed almost involuntarily. Europe's economic weight across the continent is leading it to erase progressively the political and military power of the United States by, for example, tightly surrounding with its real physical mass the American bases on the periphery of Europe.

From a strategic point of view one can look at the world in two ways: the military way suggests that the United States still exists in the Old World; the economic way reveals the increasingly marginal character of its presence, and not just in Europe but throughout Eurasia.

Within the military perspective we can repeat again the list of American installations around the world in Europe, Japan, South Korea, and elsewhere. Those who are easily impressed could say that the fifteen thousand soldiers stranded out in Uzbekistan or the twelve thousand shut up in their base in Bagram in Afghanistan are significant strategic entities. My own feeling is that these two installations are really underproductive branches of the U.S. chamber of commerce charged with distributing a few perks to the local chiefs. The latter always hold the real power, in this case the power to decide if and when to hand over the terrorists the Americans are looking for or pretending to look for. These business transactions are modest but sufficient—the underdevelopment in these regions being such that buying off local mercenaries can be done cheaply.

If we come at the questions of strategic effectiveness from an economic perspective and consider the part of the world that is experiencing real development, societies in which companies are being created and democracy instituted, such as on the edges of Europe for example, the economic and material unimportance of America has become striking.

Consider, for example, three countries on the periphery of the euro zone that are also each important strategically for the U.S. military—Turkey, a fundamental ally and the pivot between Europe, Russia, and the Middle East; Poland, a country quite understandably in a hurry to join NATO in order to definitively overcome its domination by Russia that goes back much further than the communist era; and Great Britain, America's natural ally.

Of course, we can act like the overgrown children that all military strategists are at heart and represent these three countries as strong and stable American possessions within its game to control the world. In the childlike universe of Donald Rumsfeld, for example, only physical force matters. But if we leave the military playground and consider the balance of real economic power, we see that Turkey, Poland, and Great Britain are three countries that are already within the sphere of influence of the euro zone. Great Britain trades 3.5 times more with the twelve-country Europe than with the United States, Turkey 4.5 times more, Poland 15 times more. In the event of a serious trade war between Europe and the

United States, Poland will have no choice about who to side with and Turkey will not have much choice either. As for Great Britain, any direct conflict with continental Europe will require a dose of economic heroism that is perfectly within its power.

The situation is not static. If we consider historical information concerning the years 1995–2000, we can see that Poland is already being absorbed by the euro zone. Turkey, like most countries in the world, exports a bit more to the United States than it imports. Here as elsewhere, the United States tries to play its role as omnivorous universal consumer. Despite its fundamental proximity to the sphere of European trade, Great Britain has actually moved closer to the United States in terms of trade in the last five years. The march toward the euro, poorly thought through and deflationary, was in this case more dissuasive than attractive.

An examination of these statistics shows quite clearly the force of territorial contiguity when it comes to the development of business partners. Globalization exists at two levels—one truly global, the other regional—but it implies first and foremost, as American strategic analysts have feared, a regionalization by continent or subcontinent. To the extent that it is really a global process, it has revealed the United States to be a consumer of goods and investment capital more than a positive contributor. Mathematically,

TABLE 12. Imports and Exports of Turkey, Poland, and the United Kingdom (in Millions of Dollars)

	Turkey		Poland		United Kingdom	
2000	Imports	Exports	Imports	Exports	Imports	Exports
United States	7.2	11.3	4.4	3.1	13.4	15.8
12-country						
Europe	40.8	43.4	52.3	60.0	46.6	53.5
Russia	7.1	2.3	9.4	2.7	0.7	0.4
Japan	3.0	0.4	2.2	0.2	4.7	2.0
China	2.5	0.3	2.8	0.3	2.2	0.8

SOURCE: Organization of Economic Co-operation and Development (OECD), Monthly Statistics of International Trade, November 2001.

one has to conclude that globalization's intensification of trade based on geographic contiguity will have as its most profound effect a displacement of the world's center of economic gravity toward Eurasia and an isolation of America in the New World.

The evolution of these forces, originally put in motion by the United States itself, is favoring the emergence of an integrated Europe, the de facto dominant power in a region that is strategically better situated than the one dominated by the United States. The development of Eastern Europe, Russia, Muslim countries such as Turkey or Iran, and virtually the entire Mediterranean basin would seem to make Europe a natural pole of growth and power. Its proximity to the Persian Gulf no doubt appears to America's political "thinkers" as the most dramatic threat to the country's position in the world.

Imagining the alternatives in a crisis scenario is a good way of visualizing the relative balance of power both economically and militarily. What would happen, for example, if Europe, Turkey's dominant trading partner, pressured it to not allow the American army to use the base at Incirlik in the event of a war against Iraq? What would the outcome be today? Next year? The year after? Turkey's alignment alongside Europe would cause a dramatic drop in America's military potential in the Middle East. Today's Europeans are not contemplating such scenarios, but the Americans are.

PEACE WITH RUSSIA AND THE MUSLIM WORLD

Unlike the United States, Europe has no particular problems with the outside world. It has normal commercial relations with the rest of the planet, buying the raw materials and energy that it needs and paying for these imports with the revenues earned from its exports. Its long-term strategic goal is therefore peace. American foreign policy, on the other hand, is increasingly shaped by two major conflicts with two immediate neighbors of Europe.

One is Russia, the fundamental obstacle to American hegemony but too strong to be chopped down. The other is the Muslim world, a convenient straw man opponent that serves to dramatize American military force. Since Europe's principal self-interest is peace, especially with its two biggest neighbors, its strategic priorities are now in radical opposition with those of the United States.

To the extent that the Persian Gulf countries must sell their oil because of their growing populations, Europe has no need to fear an embargo. However, it cannot accept indefinitely the continuous disorder in the Arab world sponsored by the United States and Israel. Economic realities would suggest that this region of the world will be brought within the sphere of cooperation centered in Europe and largely exclude the United States. Turkey and Iran have understood this perfectly. But make no mistake, all the ingredients are there for a serious conflict between Europe and the United States in the near future.

With Russia, a country showing every sign of becoming a sane partner—much weakened economically and militarily but still possessing huge capacities as an oil and natural gas exporter—Europe stands to multiply its ties in the years ahead. The strategic powerlessness of the United States against Russia explains in part this somewhat surprising evolution. After each round of aggressive actions the United States is obliged to make a show of friendliness toward Russia, gestures that are largely imposed by its fear that the Europeans and Russians will simply ignore the United States in future negotiations.

In the Islamic context the harm caused by America continues to worsen and is becoming ever more concrete. The Muslim world supplies Europe with a large percentage of its immigrants—Pakistanis in England, North Africans in France, and Turks in Germany to name only the three largest groups. The children of these immigrants are citizens of their host countries, including in Germany where recently created laws offering citizenship based on one's birth in the territory have brought it close to France's *"droit du sol.*" Since it is more than just a close neighbor, Europe must maintain peaceful relations and a good understanding with the Muslim world in order to insure its own internal peace. Here the United States could be seen as causing internal as well as international turmoil for Europe. With the attacks by disadvantaged Arab youths against synagogues during the early months of 2002, France was the first to experience the destabilizing effects of America's and Israel's Middle East policies even if the deeper causes of the revolt derive from the increasingly inegalitarian structure of French society itself. There is no reason to think that Germany with its Turks, and even more England with its Pakistanis, will not be affected by the destabilizing action of the United States.

THE FRANCO-GERMAN COUPLE AND ITS ENGLISH MISTRESS

To evoke Europe, its power, and its growing antagonism with the United States is to use a concept whose meaning is not clearly defined—a marketplace, a civilization, a bundle of nations. In short, it is as yet an ill-defined, evolving entity. These days the economic integration of Europe is advancing. Its size and success are attracting new members in Eastern Europe and it seems destined, despite difficulties, to eventually absorb Turkey. But this process of spontaneous economic expansion has the effect of producing increased political disorganization. Economic expansion weakens the system's institutions. The persistence of nations each with its own language, political system, and ways of thinking makes it very difficult to implement decision-making procedures that will be acceptable to all the members.

From the standpoint of global strategy, this ongoing evolution could be viewed as the beginning of a process of disintegration. In fact, it is more likely that a three-member leadership team will emerge on the continent with the United Kingdom, Germany, and France constituting this directing triumvirate. After years of misunderstanding and discord, a Franco-German partnership has become very probable. The role of the United Kingdom would be absolutely new but must be thought a possibility. We must not make the same opening mistake as Brzezinski, who assures us that Great Britain, unlike France and Germany, is not a geostrategic player. As he bluntly puts it: "Its friendship needs to be nourished, but its policies do not call for sustained attention."[5] This judgment seems rather off the mark given the recent Franco-British cooperation in elaborating a European military policy.

Between 1990 and 2001 relations between France and Germany were not good. German reunification threw Europe out of balance by creating a Germany of eighty million people that saw France shrink in relative terms with its sixty million people. Monetary union, which should have represented an optimistic step forward, was conceived to "tie" and control Germany. However, as a conciliatory gesture toward Germany, the other European states accepted exaggeratedly strict management criteria that have consigned them to years of stagnation. For its part, Germany, perhaps a bit tipsy over its newfound unity, did not play a calming role over this period, especially during the breakup of Yugoslavia. But this phase has ended. The most obvious sign is that Germany is becoming more flexible and hedonistic and could be said to be growing closer to France in its ways of thinking.

If we return to the political realist's questions concerning relationships of force, we must say that Germany's demographic crisis will inevitably place the country on a par with the other large European nations. The absolute number of births today is slightly lower than in France. In virtual terms, the two countries are the same size. The German elite are conscious of this return to a standard size. The fever of reunification has passed. Germany's leaders know that it will not be *the* great power at the heart of Europe. Specific difficulties in carrying out reconstruction in the former DDR contributed to this sobering return to reality.

For its part France is no longer paralyzed by policies that

sought to maintain the strength of the franc and has been economically liberated by the weak euro. This, along with its more favorable demographic situation, has rejuvenated France and given it new confidence. In short there are now all the ingredients for new initiatives of Franco-German cooperation to begin in a spirit of real mutual trust.

Here too, however, we ought to be mindful of the dominant role played by certain material forces. The new demographic balance was not decided on, it simply has come about through the evolution of the societies themselves and is accepted as a given by government leaders. The new Franco-German demographic equilibrium is moreover only one aspect of the worldwide demographic stabilization. To the east, Russia's demographic regression has the automatic effect of calming old German and European worries about being submerged by a demographically expanding country of its mammoth size.

Together, the demographic decline of Russia, the stagnation of Germany, and the relative health of the French population establish a new balance across Europe—and in a way that is the reverse of the process of growing instability that the continent experienced at the beginning of the twentieth century. At that time France's demographic stagnation, combined with Germany's population growth, made France into a timid nation while Russia's even more robust expansion caused a veritable phobia on the part of Germans. Birth rates are now low everywhere. This weakness causes its own specific problems, but it does have the advantage of rendering this part of the world more tranquil almost automatically. If the low birth rates persist for too long, Europe will experience a true demographic crisis that could jeopardize the continent's prosperity. At first, however, and without anyone's real awareness, the drop in demographic pressure facilitated the free-trade fusion of Europe's national economies by alleviating among the various participants their fears of political imbalance and aggression.

Any theories about the future behavior of the United Kingdom can only be wild guesses. Belonging simultaneously to two spheres, one Anglo-Saxon one European, is their natural situation.

The liberal revolution affected Great Britain more violently than any other European nation even if today the English dream of renationalizing their railroads and strengthening their health-care system with more sensible levels of budgetary support. The link between the United States and Great Britain goes much further than this narrow economic dimension. It includes the language, individualism, and a nearly congenital sense of political liberty. All of this is obvious, but it can make one forget something equally important: the English are in a better position than all other Europeans to observe not just America's faults but its evolution. If the American butter goes bad, the English will be the first to smell it. They are America's closest ally, but they are also the group most subjected to the ideological and cultural pressure that crosses the Atlantic since they do not have the natural protection that the filter of a foreign language offers the Germans, the French, and others. This is the British dilemma — not just a struggle between Europe and the United States but a problematic relationship with all things American.

One can be certain that Britain's final choice to join or reject the euro zone will be decisive, both for Europe and the United States. If the investment and banking weight of London, the leading financial pole of the Old World, is added to the euro zone, it will be a terrible blow for New York and for America, given its dependence on continuous streams of investment capital from the rest of the world. Given the present deficiencies in production of the American economy, London's entry into the European system could cause a real shift in the global balance of power. It would be a rather ironic dénouement to see the Great Britain that Brzezinski chose to ignore do in American hegemony with one blow by choosing to cast its lot with Europe.

Conclusion: Endgame

The planet is tending toward stability after the pain of an educational and demographic transition that is nearing completion. Although it experiences fits of ideological and religious fever, the Third World is on the road toward development and more democratic practices. There is no global threat that requires an emergency response by the United States to protect freedoms. Only one threat to global stability hangs over the world today—the United States itself, which was once a protector and is now a predator. At the very moment when its political and military usefulness is no longer obvious, America is realizing that it cannot do without the goods produced by the rest of the planet. But the world is too vast, too populous, too diverse, and crisscrossed by too many uncontrollable forces. No strategy, no matter how well thought out, will allow the United States to transform its semi-imperial situation into a full-fledged, legitimate empire. America is too weak economically, militarily, and ideologically. This is why every move intended to reaffirm its control over the world is causing negative blowback that weakens little by little its strategic standing.

What happened over the last dozen years? Two real empires stood face to face and one of them, the Soviet Union, fell apart. The other one, the American empire, was also engaged in a process of decomposition; however the abrupt fall of communism created the illusion that the United States had risen to a level of absolute power. After first the Soviet and then the Russian collapse, America thought it could extend its hegemony over the whole planet at the very moment when its control over its own traditional sphere was weakening.

In order to establish stable planetary hegemony there were two conditions that had to be fulfilled when it came to relations of force. First, maintain control over the European and Japanese protectorates that now constitute the poles of real economic force—the real economy being defined by production rather than consumption. Second, take out the Russians once and for all as a strategic power by achieving a total disintegration of the former Soviet sphere and the complete disappearance of a counterbalancing nuclear terror, thus leaving the United States as the sole power able to strike any country in the world unilaterally and without risk of the least reprisal.

Neither of these conditions has been accomplished. The progress of Europe toward unity and autonomy has not been stopped. Moreover, Japan has quietly kept its capacity to act alone if it should wish to do so one day. As for Russia, it is becoming more stable and, faced with the dramatic neo-imperialism of the United States, has begun modernizing its military while returning to the competition of diplomatic chess with talent and creativity.

Unable to control the real powers of its day—by holding on to Japan and Europe in the industrial sector and breaking up Russia's core and its nuclear capability—America has resorted to making a show of empire by choosing to pursue military and diplomatic actions among a series of puny powers dubbed for dramatic effect "the axis of evil" and more generally the Arab world—the point of intersection of these two axes, evil and Arab, being Iraq. In terms of its level of intensity and risk American military action is now somewhere between a real war and a video game. Embargoes are put in place against defenseless countries, insignificant armies are bombarded, increasingly sophisticated armaments that are said to have the precision of video games are being conceived and built, it is claimed, and yet in practice unarmed civilian populations are bombed in old-fashioned ways that are reminiscent of World War II. The level of risk is almost nonexistent for the American army. Risks definitely exist, however, for the American civilian population since the asymmetrical U.S. military domination causes terrorist reactions to rise up from among the dominated parts of the world—the attacks of September 11, 2001, being the most stunning example.

The ostentatious militarism of the United States, which supposedly intends to prove the technomilitary incapacity of everyone else in the world, has ended up worrying the three big real powers—Europe, Japan, and Russia—and is pushing them closer together. Herein lies the great counterproductive ricochet of America's game. America's leaders thought that at most they risked fomenting closer ties between one major power, Russia, and two minor powers, China and Iran—a scenario that would have left them in control of their Japanese and European protectorates. But what they really risk, if they do not calm down, is seeing one major nuclear power, Russia, forge closer ties with the two dominant industrial powers, Europe and Japan.

Europe is slowly becoming aware of the fact that Russia is not only no longer a strategic threat but is making a positive contribution to its military security. Who can say in all certainty that without the strategic counterweight of the Russians the United States would have permitted the creation of the euro, a terrible threat in the near term to its supply of investment capital, or the Galileo project that will breakup the American monopoly over military ground surveillance? This is the real reason why the eastward expansion of NATO is meaningless or, one should say, has a new meaning. At one time the integration of former "popular democracies" within NATO could only be interpreted as an aggressive action toward Russia, albeit strange in the context of a dignified and pacific breakup of the Soviet Union. At the time the possibility of a symbolic association of Russia within NATO was spoken of, and has now been adopted, as the face-saving presentation of an advancing process of encirclement. But now the idea of according Russia consultative status or, why not?, a decision-making role within NATO is becoming little by little a truly attractive prospect to Europeans. They would then have succeeded in formalizing within the institution a true strategic counterweight to the United States. It is easy to understand why the Americans are less and less interested in NATO and more and more interested in going it alone in their pursuit of theatrical militarism.

Controlling the oilfields of the Persian Gulf and Central Asia is obviously the rational goal of American actions in this region of weak countries. It is only superficially rational, however, since American dependence is a general problem not just an oil problem. But it is precisely in this area that the United States creates the most striking examples of negative blowback. The disquiet and agitation directly or indirectly sponsored by the United States in the Persian Gulf and its clear desire to control the energy supply on which both Europe and Japan depend can only lead these two protectorates to increasingly consider Russia, now the second-leading producer of crude oil and still the world's leading producer of natural gas, as a necessary partner.

A more systematic coordination of efforts between Europeans and the Japanese, since both are faced with the same problem of American control over their energy supply, seems increasingly certain. The similarities between the European and Japanese economies that remain industry-based can only lead to closer ties in the future. There are already signs of this as in, for example, the recent evolution of Japanese investment abroad in either the purchase or creation of businesses. In 1993 Japan invested 17.5 trillion yen in America but only 9.2 trillion in Europe. In 2000 the figures had swung the other way, with 27 trillion invested in Europe and only 13.5 trillion in North America.[1]

For anyone interested in theoretical models, recent American actions offer a marvelous opportunity to study the inevitable negative blowback that occurs when a particular strategic player sets itself a goal that is beyond its reach. Every step taken by the Americans to extend their control over the planet turns out to create new problems for them.

The game advances slowly because each of the powers, not just the United States, has several fundamental deficiencies. Europe is fragile due to its lack of unity and its demographic crisis, Russia suffers from a flat economy and its demographic woes, and Japan labors under its isolation and its own demographic problems. This is why there will be no final checkmate symbolizing the victory of one power but instead a stalemate formalizing the incapacity of any power to dominate the others. Together, Europe, Russia, and Japan are two and a half times more powerful than the United States. In the long run the strange behavior of the United States in the Muslim world will steadily push the three other powers of the northern hemisphere toward closer ties.

The world that is being created will not be an empire controlled by a single power. It will be a complex balancing act among a system of nations or metanations of the same scale even if not exactly of the same size. Some entities, such as the Russian pole, will keep a single nation at their center. The same goes for Japan, a country that appears small on the map but whose industrial production equals that of the United States and for this reason could, if it wishes, amass a technomilitary force equivalent to the U.S. force in fifteen years' time. Eventually, China will join this group.

As for Europe, it is an aggregate of nations with the Franco-German couple at its center, but its level of concrete power will depend on Britain's participation. South America seems destined to organize itself around the leadership of Brazil.

DEMOCRACIES AND OLIGARCHIES

The world born from the collapse of the Soviet empire and the breakdown of the American order will not resemble the uniformly democratic and liberal dream of Fukuyama. However, there is absolutely no way for it to revert to a Nazi-style totalitarianism, fascism, or communism. A double movement will assure the advancement of human history. The developing world is heading toward democracy—pushed by the movement toward full literacy that tends to create culturally more homogeneous societies. As for the industrialized world, it is being encroached on to varying degrees by a tendency toward oligarchy—a phenomenon that has emerged with the development of educational stratification that has divided societies into layers of "higher," "lower," and various kinds of "middle" classes.

However, we must not exaggerate the antidemocratic effects of this unegalitarian educational stratification. Developed countries, even if they become more oligarchical, remain literate countries and will have to deal with the contradictions and conflicts that could arise between a democratically leaning literate mass and university-driven stratification that favors oligarchical elites.

The establishment of a neoprotectionist system on the level of the large regions or metanations defined above would strengthen the democratic tendency by favoring workers and engineers when it comes to economic activity and the distribution of the national or metanational income.

Since it tends to widen income gaps, absolute free trade would, on the other hand, lead to the triumph of oligarchy. American control of the system would lead to the kind of situation of which we have seen signs in the years 1995 to 2000—the transformation of the American people into an imperial society of plebeians nourished on the industrial goods produced by the rest of the world. But as I have tried to show, the complete achievement of this latter scenario is quite unlikely.

UNDERSTANDING BEFORE ACTING

What can citizens and elected officials do given the fact that to a great extent we are carried along by economic, sociological, and historical forces beyond our control?

First, we can learn to look at the world as it is, wrest ourselves from the hold of ideology, the illusion of the moment, and the media's permanent false alarm as Nietzsche used to say. To perceive the real relations of force is an important first step. At least it gives one the opportunity to avoid the most counterproductive actions. America is not a super superpower or "hyperpuissance." At the moment it can only terrorize weak nations. When it comes to the real global matchups, it is at the mercy of a mutual understanding between Europeans, Russians, and Japanese. The latter have in theory the possibility to strangle it. The United States is unable to live on its own economic activity and must be subsidized to maintain its level of consumption—at its present cruising speed that subsidy amounts to 1.4 billion dollars per day (as of April 2003).[2] If its behavior continues to be disruptive, it is America that ought to fear an embargo.

Some American strategists are, I fear, more aware than their European counterparts of just how strategically sensitive some of their decisions are. The euro, in particular, though born amidst conflicts and uncertainty, will, if it holds on, be a permanent threat to the American system. Its existence puts in place a critical economic mass of a size comparable or superior to that of the United

States' dollar zone—one capable of taking concerted action in a particular direction with enough force to upset former equilibria and be especially disturbing to the already imbalanced American system.

Before the euro the United States could count on certain asymmetrical advantages no matter what it did. The ups and downs of the dollar had worldwide repercussions. The smaller currencies adjusted as best they could but had no effect on the United States. Now, however, America can be seriously affected by one-way global movements—for example, the fall of the euro from the day of its creation until February 2002. This process, unbidden and unforeseen, most certainly corresponded to a flight of capital toward the United States, but it also had the effect of lowering European prices by 25 percent. The euro had in effect established a tariff barrier. To protest afterward about America's decision to raise customs duties on foreign steel is rather disingenuous on the part of Europeans. Worse, it reveals an ignorance as to their real power. The masters are protesting as though they were servants. The recovery of the euro could symmetrically favor American industry, but, on the other hand, it would also cause the supply of investment capital to dry up abruptly.

The existence of the euro will lead to more economic cooperation between European nations and to the invention of a common fiscal policy. Indeed, if this does not happen, the euro will disappear. But Europeans should understand that the emergence of a fiscal policy for the entire continent would have worldwide macroeconomic consequences, including the breakup of the American monopoly over the regulation of the business cycle. If, for example, the Europeans decided to launch a global stimulus policy, they would at the same time annihilate the only real service rendered by the United States, namely that of being the gigantic Keynesian consumer propping up demand.

I would not venture to speculate in so few pages about the countless effects and interactions that such a change in behavior would bring about for international investment flows, commercial activity, and worldwide immigration. But the overall result is easy to predict: a regulatory pole will emerge in Eurasia, one closer to the geographic center of the world, and there will be a slowdown in the flow of goods, capital, and migration that currently nourishes the United States. The United States will then have to live like other nations, notably by reigning in its huge trade deficit, a constraint that would imply a 15 to 20 percent drop in the standard of living of the population. This figure is based on the principle that only imported and exported merchandise has international value. The majority of "goods and services" currently tabulated within the American GNP have no value on international markets and are therefore heavily overvalued.

The prospect of this adjustment has nothing terrifying about it. This drop in the standard of living is nothing compared to the 50 percent freefall experienced by Russia at the end of the communist period, a fall that started from a GNP that was already significantly lower than that of the United States. The American economy is flexible by nature, and one can confidently imagine a rapid adaptation that would be beneficial to the global system. The negative observations about present trends should not obscure the intrinsic strengths of America, whether one thinks of its economic flexibility or its attachment to principles of political liberty. Thinking reasonably about America in no way means trying to get rid of it, diminish it, or undertake any other fantasy-filled violence toward it. What the world needs is not that America disappear but that it return to its true self—democratic, liberal, and productive. Of course I mean *as much as possible*, since in human history, as with the rest of the animal world, it is never actually possible to go back completely to previous conditions. Dinosaurs have not come back, and the authentically imperial and generous America of the 1950s will not come back either.

Besides training ourselves to acquire an accurate perception of the reality of the world, what can we do? I would say modestly act on the margins to facilitate a transition that will come about mostly on its own. Given the current relations of economic, demographic, and cultural force in the world, no system of international politics can change the course of history. One can only try to facilitate the emergence of a reasonable political superstructure while avoiding as best one can violent confrontations.

The existence of a mutually terrifying nuclear threat is still necessary given the current state of uncertainty of American society and its economy. It matters little whether this balance of terror is maintained by the Russians or by the implementation of a European nuclear deterrent force.

Since they have the money to pay for their imports, Europe and Japan should speak directly with Russia, Iran, and the Arab world about the stable delivery of the oil and gas they need. They have no reason to engage in American-style theatrical military interventionism.

The United Nations, both as an incarnation of a certain ideology and as a political organization, must be the instrument for carrying out these large-scale general adjustments. In this regard the United States' hostility toward the United Nations is a sign of its correct awareness of the organization's threat to its interests. To make this great international organization more effective, it will be necessary for those involved to do a better job at taking into formal account the real relations of economic force. Today's world war is fought through a continuous network of economic battles, and it is therefore an aberration that the two major industrial nations of Japan and Germany are not permanent members of the Security Council. This exclusion is simply a sign of their continued submission to the American order.

Demanding a seat on the Security Council for Japan is merely common sense. Being the only country to have suffered a nuclear attack, and now fundamentally pacifist, Japan has a deeply legitimate claim on our serious attention. Its economic conceptions, which differ markedly from those in the Anglo-Saxon world, can only be a useful counterweight for the entire planet. For Germany the solution is not so easy because the European nations are already overrepresented, proportionately speaking, on the Security Council and it would be improper to exacerbate this imbalance by claiming yet one more seat. This is an opportunity for France to play smart and offer to share its seat with Germany. A jointly held Franco-German seat would have much more influence than the current seat and add considerable weight to any exercise of their veto power.

Moving the headquarters of certain international organizations from the United States to Eurasia would also contribute to a realignment of the global political superstructure with the emerging economic reality in the world. However, the creation of new international organizations would no doubt be simpler and cause fewer conflicts than relocating, say, the International Monetary Fund or the World Bank, two institutions that are largely discredited today in the minds of many.

These proposals for action are nothing more than initiatives for bringing institutional forms in line with the essential consciousness of the economic relations of force in the world. If the planet is moving toward greater stability and peace through the interaction of demographic, cultural, social, and political forces, no grand strategy is really necessary. We must not forget two important related truths: as in the past, the true forces today are linked to demographics and education, and true power is economic power. It serves no purpose to lose one's way in a real or imaginary military competition with the United States that would require endless incursions within countries of no real strategic importance. We should not follow America's military leaders for whom the term "theatre of operations" has ceased being a metaphor. Fighting alongside the Americans in Iraq would only amount to playing a small role in a bloody vaudeville show.

In the twentieth century no country succeeded in increasing its power through military buildups or war. France, Germany, Japan, and Russia all suffered heavy losses at that game. Americans came out of the twentieth century winners because for a very long time they knew how to refuse getting too involved in military conflicts in the Old World. Let us follow the example of that early successful America. Let us dare to become strong by refusing militarism and concentrating instead on the economic and social problems within our societies. Let the present America expend what remains of its energy, if that is what it wants to do, on "war on terrorism"—a substitute battle for the perpetuation of a hegemony that it has already lost. If it stubbornly decides to continue showing off its supreme power, it will only end up exposing to the world its powerlessness.

NOTES

Introduction

1. Norman Podhoretz, "How to Win World War IV," *Commentary* (February 2002): 19–28.
2. Todd is alluding to an influential essay by Montaigne's best friend, Etienne de la Boétie (1530–1563) entitled *Discours de la servitude volontaire* (1576).
3. See Joseph S. Nye, *The Paradox of American Power: Why the World's Only Superpower Can't Go It Alone* (Oxford: Oxford University Press, 2003).
4. Cf. Noam Chomsky, *Rogue States: The Rule of Force in World Affairs* (London: Pluto Press, 2000).
5. Benjamin R. Barber, *Jihad vs. McWorld: How Globalism and Tribalism Are Reshaping the World* (New York: Ballantine Books, 1995).
6. Henry Kissinger, *Does America Need a Foreign Policy?: Toward a Diplomacy for the 21st Century*, (New York: Simon and Schuster, 2001).
7. Paul Kennedy, *The Rise and Fall of Great Powers: Economic Change and Military Conflict from 1500 to 2000* (London: Fontana Press, 1989 [1988]).
8. Samuel P. Huntington, *The Clash of Civilizations and the Remaking of World Order* (London: Touchstone Books, 1998 [1996]).
9. Robert Gilpin, *Global Political Economy: Understanding the International Economic Order* (Princeton: Princeton University Press, 2001).
10. Zbigniew Brzezinski, *The Grand Chessboard: American Primacy and Its Geostrategic Imperatives* (New York: Basic Books, 1997).
11. Francis Fukuyama, *The End of History and the Last Man* (London: Penguin, 1992) (in French, *La Fin de l'histoire et le dernier homme* [Paris: Flammarion, 1992]).
12. Fukayama, *End of History*, p. 116. Education appears as a consequence of industrial society.
13. Michael Doyle, "Kant: Liberal Legacies and Foreign Policy," *Philosophy and Public Affairs*, 1 and 2, no. 12 (1983): 205–235, 323–353.
14. Translator's note: The author is alluding to an essay by the German philosopher Immanuel Kant (1724–1804) entitled *Project for a Perpetual Peace* (1915, 1972) (in German, *Zum ewigen Frieden*, 1795, 2^{d} ed. 1796).

15. "If we have to use force, it is because we are America. We are the indispensable nation. We stand tall, and we see further into the future." Madeleine Albright speaking about Iraq on NBC's "Today" show, February 19, 1998.

16. Michael Lind, *The Next American Nation: The New Nationalism and the Fourth American Revolution* (New York: The Free Press, 1995).

17. Translator's note: Todd is referring here to the two-round electoral system used at many levels of French government, including the presidency. In the latest presidential election, in the spring of 2002, the center-right incumbent, Jacques Chirac, received slightly more votes than the far-right candidate, Jean-Marie Le Pen, who in turn edged out the center-left candidate, Lionel Jospin. The rules state that when no candidate has a clear majority after the first round, a second run-off takes place two weeks later between the two top candidates, in this case Chirac and Le Pen, each with roughly 20 percent of the vote after the first round (hence Todd's numbers). In the second round Chirac benefited from a huge negative campaign against the far-right candidate, which therefore makes the figure of 82 percent hardly indicative of the levels of actual support for Chirac himself. One might add that, just as the background and sympathies of those who voted for Chirac were not uniform, the 20 percent of the vote won by Le Pen is not indicative of his true popularity either, since it also included uncertain amounts of negative voters and in any case is not composed of a single mass of France's most indigent or least educated as Todd's expression "*20% d'en bas*" might suggest.

18. Michael Young, *The Rise of the Meritocracy* (Harmondsworth, U.K.: Penguin, 1961 [1958]).

19. Lind, *Next American Nation*, 145.

1: The Myth of Universal Terrorism

1. Translator's note: "*banlieue*," translated here as "suburb," has the same negative connotation in French that "inner-city" has for an American reader. It should be noted that, unlike America where the underclass is often concentrated in the least desirable parts of urban centers, in France the lower classes have been relegated to the suburbs, thus leaving the "*centre ville*" highly attractive to tourists and convention organizers with all the attendant economic payoffs.

2. There is a substantial Chinese minority in Malaysia.

3. There is a substantial Christian minority in Nigeria.

4. Youssef Courbage, "Israel et Palestine: Combien d'hommes demain?" *Population et sociétés* 362 (November 2000). The ultra-Orthodox birth rate alone is 7.0.

5. Pierre Manent, *Les Libéraux* (Paris: Gallimard (Collection "Tel"), 2001).
6. For a general analysis of these interactions in English, see E. Todd, *The Causes of Progress: Culture, Authority and Change* (London: Blackwell, 1987), originally published as *L'Enfance du monde: Structures familiales et développement* (Paris: Le Seuil, 1984). See also Todd's *L'Invention de l'Europe* (Paris: Le Seuil, 1990).
7. Emannuel Todd, *La Chute finale*, Paris: Seuil, 1976. Translated as *The Final Fall: An Essay on the Decomposition of the Soviet Sphere*, New York: Karz, 1979).
8. See Jean-Claude Chesnais, "La Transition démographique," *Cahier de l'INED* (Paris: PUF, 1986), 122, n. 13. Translated by Philip Kreager as *The Demographic Transition: Stages, Patterns, and Economic Implications* (Oxford: Oxford University Press, 2001).
9. Gilles Kepel, *Jihad: Expansion et déclin de l'islamisme* (Paris: Gallimard, 2000), 2^d ed. Rev. (Folio), 2003). In English, *Jihad: The Trail of Political Islam*, trans. Anthony F. Roberts (Cambridge: Harvard University Press, 2003) for the second edition.
10. As so often happens, the Civil War erupted during a time of lowering birth rates among the Anglo-Saxon population in America. More Americans died in this war (620,000, of which 360,000 were Union soldiers) than in all other wars combined that America has fought, including Vietnam.
11. On the evolution of birth rates in this region, see J.-P. Sardon, "Transition et fécondité dans les Balkans socialistes," in B. Kotzamanis and A. Parant, eds., *L'Europe des Balkans, différente et diverse?* (Colloque de Bari, June 2001, Réseau Démo Balk) (Bari: Universitata degli studi di Bari, Facolta di scienze politiche, June 2001).

2: Democracy as a Threat

1. Translator's note: The above quotation comes from the first paragraph of Part II of Book 6 of Aristotle's *Politics* (350 B.C.), here translated by Benjamin Jowett: "The basis of a democratic state is liberty; which, according to the common opinion of men, can only be enjoyed in such a state; this they affirm to be the great end of every democracy. One principle of liberty is for all to rule and be ruled in turn, and indeed democratic justice is the application of numerical not proportionate equality; whence it follows that the majority must be supreme, and that whatever the majority approve must be the end and the just. Every citizen, it is said, must have equality, and therefore in a democracy the poor have more power than the rich, because there are more of them, and the will of the majority is supreme. This, then, is one

note of liberty which all democrats affirm to be the principle of their state. Another is that a man should live as he likes. This, they say, is the privilege of a freeman, since, on the other hand, not to live as a man likes is the mark of a slave. This is the second characteristic of democracy, whence has arisen the claim of men to be ruled by none, if possible, or, if this is impossible, to rule and be ruled in turns; and so it contributes to the freedom based upon equality."

2. Translator's note: Marie-Jean-Antoine-Nicolas de Caritat, Marquis de Condorcet (1743–1794), was a French philosopher of the Enlightenment and advocate of educational reform. He was one of the major revolutionary formulators of the ideas of progress, or the indefinite perfectibility of mankind. His best-known work is the *Esquisse d'un tableau historique des progrès de l'esprit humain*, 1795 (Paris: Vrin, 1970)—*Sketch for a Historical Picture of the Progress of the Human Mind.*

3. Translator's note: Alexis de Tocqueville (1805–1859) was a French political scientist, historian, and politician, best known for his *Democracy in America* (*De la Démocratie en Amérique*, 1835–40), a perceptive analysis of the political and social system of the United States in the early nineteenth century. On the basis of observations, readings, and discussions with a host of eminent Americans during his nine-month visit (1831–1832), Tocqueville attempted to penetrate directly to the essentials of American society and to highlight that aspect—equality of conditions—that was most relevant to his own philosophy. Tocqueville's study analyzed the vitality, the excesses, and the potential future of American democracy. Above all, the work was infused with his message that a society, properly organized, could hope to retain liberty in a democratic social order. Source: Seymour Drescher, *Encyclopedia Britannica.*

4. Translated as *The Explanation of Ideology: Family Structures and Social Systems*, (London: Blackwell, 1985).

5. For further details, see my *Explanation of Ideology*, chapter 5. The Muslims of Yugoslavia, Albania, and Kazakstan are patrilineal, communitarian, and egalitarian but not endogamous. The Muslims of Malaysia and Indonesia have an entirely different system that includes a higher status for women, evident, for example, in the custom that after marriage the new household tends to establish itself in close proximity to the wife's family.

6. In 1853, in a letter to Gustave de Beaumont, De Tocqueville defined popular Russia as "America without the Enlightenment thinkers and liberty. A scary democratic society." Alexis de Tocqueville, *Oeuvres complètes*, vol. 8, *Correspondance d'Alexis de Tocqueville et de Gustave de Beaumont* (Paris: Gallimard, 1967), vol. 3, p. 164.

7. The birth rate of African Americans and Latin Americans is 2.1.

3: Imperial Dimensions

1. Translator's note: Following the victory at the Battle of Salamis during the Persian Wars, the Ionian cities joined together in the Delian League for mutual protection. They placed Athens at the head (*hegemon*) because of her naval supremacy and because many of the Greek cities were annoyed with the tyrannical behavior of the Spartan commander Pausanias, who had been leader of the Greeks during the Persian War. This free confederation (*symmachia*) of autonomous cities, founded in 478 B.C., consisted of representatives, an admiral, and treasurers appointed by Athens. It was called the Delian League because its treasury was located at Delos. An Athenian leader, Aristides, initially assessed the allies in the Delian League 460 talents a year to be paid to the treasury, either in cash or ships. Source: The Historynet: http://ancienthistory.about.com/library/ weekly/aa070402a.html

2. For more information, see Russell Meiggs, *The Athenian Empire* (Oxford: Oxford University Press, 1979).

3. See G. Alföldy, *Histoire sociale de Rome* (Paris: Picard, 1991). Here is an extract from the above-mentioned passage of Artistotle's *Politics*, also from the Jowett translation: "But a city ought to be composed, as far as possible, of equals and similars; and these are generally the middle classes. Wherefore the city which is composed of middle-class citizens is necessarily best constituted in respect of the elements of which we say the fabric of the state naturally consists. And this is the class of citizens which is most secure in a state, for they do not, like the poor, covet their neighbors' goods; nor do others covet theirs, as the poor covet the goods of the rich; and as they neither plot against others, nor are themselves plotted against, they pass through life safely. Wisely then did Phocylides pray — 'Many things are best in the mean; I desire to be of a middle condition in my city.' "

4. Translator's note: *The American Heritage Dictionary* defines "Bread and Circuses" as offerings, such as benefits or entertainments, intended to placate discontent or distract attention from a policy or situation. The expression is a translation of "panem et circenses," a phrase coined by the Roman poet Juvenal (c. 60–140).

5. U.S. Trade Balance with Advanced Technology, U.S. Census Bureau, http://www.census.gov/foreign-trade/balance/c0007.html

6. Arnold Toynbee, et al., *Le monde en mars 1939* (Paris: Gallimard, 1958).

7. Chalmers Johnson, *Blowback: The Costs and Consequences of American Empire* (New York: Henry Holt, 2000). See p. 197 for Johnson's discussion of the structural implosion of demand.

8. Joseph E. Stiglitz, *Globalization and Its Discontents* (New York: Norton, 2002).

9. Translator's note: John Maynard Keynes (1883–1946) was an English economist, journalist, and financier. He is best known for his revolutionary economic theories (Keynesian economics) on the causes of prolonged unemployment. His most important work, *The General Theory of Employment, Interest and Money* (1935–36), advocated a remedy for economic recession based on a government-sponsored policy of full employment. Source: Robert Lekachman, *Encyclopedia Britannica*. For Keynes's kind word about the pharaohs, see p. 131 of Vol. 7 of the *Collected Writings of John M. Keynes*, (London: Macmillan and Cambridge University Press, 1973).

10. It can hardly be an accident that for the first time Hollywood has produced a major motion toga picture (*Gladiator*, 2000) that is generally sympathetic to the Roman Empire although critical of its degenerate "bread and circuses" phase. The ideological position of this film is significantly different from earlier anti-Roman films such as *Quo Vadis?*, *Spartacus*, or *Ben Hur*.

11. Translator's note: Friedrich List (1789–1846) was a noted German economist. Todd refers to a recent French translation of his major work from 1840: *Système national d'économie politique*, new ed. (Paris: Gallimard (Collection "Tel"), 2000). In English, *National System of Political Economy: The Theory*, trans. Sampson S. Lloyd (Dry Bones Press, 1999).

12. Michael Lind, *The Next American Nation* (New York: The Free Press, 1995). In 1984 campaign contributions to the Democratic party from business leaders were higher than those from workers' unions (see p. 187).

13. Ibid, p. 231.

4: The Fragility of Tribute

1. See Basil Henry Liddell Hart et al., *History of the Second World War* (New York: DeCapo Press, 1999 [1973]).

2. The following statistics are not broken down by front and theater of operations, but the overall numbers of combat deaths confirm my summary of the situation: United States (against Germany and Japan) 300,000 deaths; Great Britain 260,000; France 250,000; Russia 13,000,000; Japan (against all enemies) 1,750,000; Germany 3,250,000.

3. U.S. Census Bureau, *Statistical Abstract of the United States*, 2000, table 580.

4. Translator's note: In the spring of 2002 Dassault Aviation, an important French aeronautics company and defense contractor, lost out to an American rival, Boeing, in its bid to supply military aircraft to South Korea. Das-

sault executives were upset that what was billed as a fair and open competition seemed quite clearly to have been rigged for political reasons to preserve the strategic relationship between the United States and South Korea.

5. Interview in Échos, April 11, 2002.

6. Felix Rohatyn, "The Betrayal of Capitalism," *The New York Review of Books*, January 31, 2002.

7. Translator's note: The German sociologist Max Weber (1864–1920) claimed that what ultimately defines the state is its monopoly on "legitimate domination." See Max Weber's *Economy and Society* (*Wirtschaft und Gesellschaft*, 1922), edited by Guenther Roth and Claus Wittich (New York: Bedminister Press, 1968), vol. 1, *Conceptual Exposition*, 212–54. For a brief discussion of Weber's types of authority see http://www2.pfeiffer.edu/~lridener/ DSS/Weber/ WEBERW5.HTML

8. Bureau of Economic Analysis, *U.S. International Transaction Account Data*.

9. Translator's note: Adam Smith (1723–1790), *The Wealth of Nations* (London: Penguin, 1979 [1776]), p. 430. In the economic sense intended by Smith, the word *servant* would no doubt include a large amount of the new American service-oriented economy.

10. Translator's note: Todd is alluding to the title of the front-page editorial in *Le Monde* for September 12, 2001—"Nous sommes tous américains." This title and the claim it makes gave rise to heated debates in the days and weeks that followed its publication. For a partial review of this commotion, including the full text of the editorial in question, see Jean-Marie Colombani, *Tous Américains?: Le monde après le 11 septembre*, Paris: Fayard, 2002. Mr. Colombani is the director of the daily newspaper *Le Monde*.

5: The Movement Away from Universalism

1. Translator's note: Edward E. Evans-Pritchard (1902–1973) was professor of social anthropology at the University of Oxford from 1946 to 1970. His major works include: *Witchcraft, Oracles and Magic among the Azande* (1937), *The Nuer* (1940), and *African Political Systems* (1940) with Meyer Fortes. Meyer Fortes (1906–1983) studied under Charles Seligman, Bronislaw Malinowski, and Raymond Firth, and he later collaborated with A. R. Radcliffe-Brown, E. E. Evans-Pritchard, and Max Gluckman. A structural-funcionalist and Africanist with a background in psychology, Fortes's work is said to have set the standard for all subsequent studies of African social organization. He chaired the anthropology department at Cambridge University from 1950 to

1973. His major works include *The Dynamics of Clanship among the Tallensi* (1945) and *The Web of Kinship among the Tallensi* (1959).

2. I will develop this point further in a forthcoming study entitled, *The Origin of Family Systems*. I will show the relatively archaic status, anthropologically speaking, of the Anglo-Saxon family. This anthropological archaism makes no judgments about the potential for cultural and economic development in areas that have this form as a dominant family pattern. I will also demonstrate that some highly evolved family patterns, again in an anthropological sense, such as the Chinese or Arab forms, can obstruct development.

3. Op. Cit. E. Todd, *La Chute finale*.

4. American census statistics identify five groups of citizens: Whites, Blacks, Hispanics, Asians, and Indians. At present, given the fact that Indians are a relatively small population and, like the Asians, mixed into the general population through intermarriage with individuals from other groups, they ought to be considered as unproblematic pseudogroups that help mask the more pointed "statistical segregation" of blacks and Hispanics.

5. Source: http://www.census.gov/population/projections/nations/summary

6. With characteristic opportunism, the neoconservative journal *Commentary*, published by the American Jewish Committee, did not reveal in its review of Huntington's book his exclusion of Israel outside of the Western sphere. See *The Clash of Civilizations and the Remaking of World Order*, by Samuel P. Huntington, reviewed by Richard Pipes, *Commentary* (March 1997): 62–65.

7. The American Jewish Committee, 2001 *Annual Survey of American Jewish Opinion*, http://www.ajc.org

8. Aristotle, *Politics*, book 5, 7, (14), Paris: Les Belles Lettres, 1989, 64–65.

9. See the remarkable essay by Ilan Greilsammer, "Clivages et Fractures," *Le Débat* 118, (January-February 2002): 117–131.

10. When I wrote these lines in the spring of 2002, my eye happened to fall on a report in the French newspaper *Libération* about an interview with Jean-Marie Le Pen published in the Israeli newspaper *Haaretz*. In the *Haaretz* interview Le Pen, the leader of the far-right party in France, expresses his sympathy for the antiterrorist and anti-Arab campaign led by the Israeli army, Tsahal, which he compares to battles fought by the French army in Algeria four decades earlier. *Libération*, April 22, 2002.

11. See Peter Novick, *The Holocaust in American Life* (Boston: Houghton Mifflin, 1999).

12. Consider, for example, the cover of the conservative newspaper *The Weekly Standard* the day after the first round in the last French presidential elec-

tions. Against the background of the French flag appear the words "Liberté, Égalité, Judéophobie." May 6, 2002.

6: Confront the Strong or Attack the Weak?

1. Michael Porter, *The Competitive Advantage of Nations* (New York: Macmillan, 1990).
2. Lester Thurow, *Head to Head: The Coming Economic Battle Among Japan, Europe, and America* (New York: William Morrow and Nicholas Brealey, 1993).
3. For an excellent account of this period, see Jacques Sapir, *Le Chaos russe* (Paris: La Découverte, 1996).
4. In theory, there is a way that would allow for a birth rate of two children per woman and absolutely respect the patrilineal preference—if every couple stopped having children as soon as they had a son and kept trying until they did. But this is a very idealistic hypothesis that has the added disadvantage of denying the possibility of having two sons, thus eliminating another dimension of the traditional Arab family, namely the solidarity between brothers and the preference for marriages uniting their children; i.e., first cousins.

7: The Return of Russia

1. OECD, *Economic Surveys 2001–2002, Russian Federation*, vol. 2002/5.
2. Robert Gilpin, *Global Political Economy* (Princeton: Princeton University Press, 2001), 333–339.
3. Paris: Robert Laffont (Collection "Bouquin"), 1990.
4. Olivier Roy, *La Nouvelle Asie centrale ou la fabrication des nations* (Paris: Le Seuil, 1997).
5. Olivier Roy, *La Nouvelle Asie centrale*, op. cit.; *L'Asie centrale contemporaine* (Paris: Presses Universitaires de France, 2001).
6. La Documentation française, *Le Courrier des pays de l'Est* 1020 (November-December 2001): 175.
7. U.S. Census Bureau, http://www.census.gov/foreign-trade/balance/c4623.html

8: The Emancipation of Europe

1. Translator's note: Todd is referring again to the Jean-Marie Colombani editorial in *Le Monde* for September 12, 2001, entitled "Nous sommes tous américains." The other Jean-Marie mentioned above is a French entrepre-

neur whose enthusiasm for things American, along with his spectacular rise
and fall within the "empire" of Vivendi-Universal, has been the subject of
intense media attention in France.

2. L. Long, "Residential Mobility Differences Among Developed Countries,"
International Regional Science Review 14, no. 2 (1991): 133–147.

3. Anthony King, "Distrust of Government: Explaining American Exception-
alism," in Susan J. Pharr and Robert D. Putnam, eds., *Disaffected Democracies* (Princeton University Press, 2000), pp. 74–98.

4. Translator's note: A French engineer, economist, and sociologist, Frédéric
Le Play (1806–1882) is remembered politically for his defense of conservative
and traditionalist reforms that sought to reinstate the authority of property
owners, factory owners, and fathers. Among family sociologists he is considered a pioneer in the empirical analysis of family customs and budgets.

5. Brzezinski, op. cit., p. 43.

Conclusion: Endgame

1. Source: http://www.jin.jac.02.jp/stat/stats/08TRA42.html

2. Translator's note: For more recent discussions of these issues in the Ameri-
can press, see William Finnegan, "The Economics of Empire: Notes on the
Washington Consensus," *Harper's Magazine* (May 2003): 41–54 and Niall
Ferguson, "True Cost of Hegemony: Huge Debt," *New York Times*, April 20,
2003, section 4, pp. 1, 5. Ferguson is also the author of *Empire: The Rise and
Demise of the British World Order and the Lessons for Global Power* (New
York: Basic Books, 2003).

INDEX